GOD'S
PROPHETIC
FEASTS

*The Joy and Importance
of Seasonal Celebrations*

Jacob Keegstra

ISBN 978-965-7542-10-1

Lay-out: Petra van der Zande

Photos: ICEJ and Internet (free domain)

Printed in Jerusalem by PRINTIV

Published by: Tsur Tsina Publications
Email: tsurtsinapublications@gmail.com

ICEJ  INTERNATIONAL CHRISTIAN EMBASSY JERUSALEM **International Christian Embassy Jerusalem**
PO Box 1192, Jerusalem, 91010, Israel

Website: http://int.icej.org

CONTENTS

CONTENTS

FOREWORD

God is the creator of time. He is the beginning and the end and what is even more exciting, he knows the end before the beginning. When He created the world, he determined that our time would pass in repetitive annual circles. "While the earth remains, Seedtime and harvest, Cold and heat, Winter and summer, And day and night Shall not cease." (Genesis 8:22)

When God transmitted his word through the Jewish people to human mankind He appointed for every year certain seasons when He as the creator of heaven and earth would meet with His people Israel. "Three times a year all your males shall appear before the LORD your God in the place which He chooses: at the Feast of Unleavened Bread, at the Feast of Weeks, and at the Feast of Tabernacles; and they shall not appear before the LORD empty-handed." (Deuteronomy 16:16)

The Hebrew term *Mo'ed* is usually translated as feast. But *Mo'ed* more correctly implies a pre-appointed time of meeting. This means there were three nonnegotiable annual calendar entries for every Jew to meet with God.

Each time there was ample reason for thanksgiving as each meeting related to the various harvest seasons. But also each feast reminded Israel on important truths regarding the character and purpose of God.

While we Christians appreciate the fulfilment of Passover and Pentecost in the New Testament, many of us are unaware of the prophetic significance of the feast of Tabernacles for the Jewish people and the church.

In this unique and much needed study of "God's prophetic feasts" Jacob Keegstra lines out from Genesis to Revelation the prophetic line-up of God's purposes with humanity.

This well researched book will for sure be blessing for every reader as it unfolds God's great plans for Israel and the Nations – past, present and future.

My prayer is that as you read this book, that this also will become a personal *Mo'ed*, a personal date between you and God.

May the Lord bless you as you prayerfully read and study God's prophetic Feasts.

Dr. Jürgen Bühler

Executive Director
International Christian Embassy Jerusalem
Jerusalem, July 2012

Chapter 1

Celebrating the Future with God

Introduction

In the beginning God created the heavens and the earth. From time immemorial human beings have been transfixed by the majesty of God revealed in his starry heavens and have followed the sun and the moon in particular, as they move inevitably through the seasons of the year. In addition, we have now come to mark on our calendars fixed times or festivals of celebration such as Christmas and Easter, or the end of summer and the beginning of the fall season.[a]

Everyone knows from experience that a week is divided into seven days with six days of work and one day of rest. It is God's way of building in moments of work and moments of reflection. God has also divided the year into moments of celebration and commemoration by establishing feasts or festive days. By celebrating these kinds of festivals year after year, people are reminded of the things God has done for them in the past, and hopefully will do for them in the future.[b] [1]

What are festivals beyond the wonderful preparation of food, gathering together of friends and family, often accompanied by the giving of gifts? Do feasts merely help us commemorate the past and present[2] or do they also point forward towards the future?[3]

What is the future nature of feasts? There are practically no references foretelling the precise nature of these feasts.[4] On the other hand, Christian theological literature about the future gives us many references to the coming century such as 'Olam HaBa', the Day of the Lord, the Kingdom of God or the Wedding of the Lamb.

---

[a] Genesis 1:14   [b] Exodus 34:24; Deuteronomy 16:16,17

Could the yearning for the Coming Age have something to do with festive days, that is, with celebrating the Feasts of the Lord?

We know from reading the Old Testament that God's people celebrated the Feast of Tabernacles at two important moments in their history, that is, at the Dedication of the Temple and after the Exile.[a] I believe that God's great acts of salvation are connected with great acts of celebration.

Let's begin our study of these feasts. First let's look at how they were developed as they were outlined in the Old Testament. Once we have examined how the Old Testament describes the background of the feasts we will move on to the New Testament views, that is, how did Jesus Christ interpret the feasts? How did the feasts affect the Christian tradition?

Are there elements of the feasts that will not be fulfilled until Christ's return?

These questions together with some possible answers can help us understand the significance of these feasts. Our ultimate goal is to know whether these festivals have a prophetic dimension, and how certain events may unfold. Do the feasts in their very structure give us clues, some hint, to an ultimate future festival?

In other words:

"What is the prophetic significance of the Feasts of the Lord?"

---

[a] 1 Kings 8; Nehemiah 8

Chapter 2

Background to our Approach

If you are like most people today you may be a very busy person who may not have the time to read through the entire book. So I have also designed this book for easy reading. You can, if you wish, skip Chapters 2 and 3 which are largely theological in nature and move straight on to Chapter 4 which focuses on Spring Festivals. If you have the time to read through — and think through with me — the theological framework in Chapters 2 and 3 then let's begin.

There are various traditions or strains contained in Christian theological literature that deal with feasts. These traditions are based on different premises but the fundamental premise out of which my argument springs is that God reveals himself[5] in history as it has been described in both the Old and the New Testament.[6] And consequently we can interpret the Word of God primarily from two related perspectives: an historical point of view as well as a literal point of view.[7] In this respect, the relationship between the Old and New Testament is significant.[8]

For example, the New Testament apostles proclaim the gospel of Jesus Christ to be a fulfilment of the Old Testament.[9] So, can we really characterize the Old Testament as a promise or a prophecy?[10] I believe that first and foremost prophecy is a proclamation, a proclamation of a topical (an historical) event. Secondly prophecy contains a future promise which we should never separate from its original history.[11] In other words, the prophetic Word of God is historical, that is, it rooted in the history of God's dealings with his people and it is simultaneously prophetic or eschatological, that is, it foreshadows future events to come.

The Future Consummation
The majority of the Old Testament promises, I believe, have been fulfilled in Jesus Christ in the New Testament but several Old Testament promises

concerning the future remain unfulfilled. The New Testament testifies to the testimony of Jesus and his testimony is the spirit of prophecy.[a]

In addition the New Testament adds an eschatological perspective. The partial fulfilment of an Old Testament promise in the New Testament confirms that the rest of the promise will one day be fulfilled.[12] In other words, the New Testament absorbs the Old Testament prophecy and then transcends it.[13]

The ultimate fulfilment of this prophecy as an historical reality is the completion of what has become, for the moment, only a partial reality in the New Testament.[14] We can characterize therefore the Word of God in the Old and New Testament in three ways as Promise, Fulfilment and Consummation.[15]

I believe that Jesus Christ fulfils the Old Testament prophecy, a promise which is to be consummated in the future[b] [16] that is Jesus has already come into this world as an historical reality: his incarnation lies at the heart of the Christian message. Prophecy foretells an historical incarnation in time and space; the future is not a timeless idea or concept existing outside of history as suggested by the German theological school of Karl Barth.[17]

In theological literature a great deal of importance is placed on the **fact** or the **place** of salvation but I believe that insufficient emphasis is placed on the importance of the **time** of salvation.[18]

Let's consider how important time is in God's redemptive plan in order to gain a better understanding of the nature and significance of God's feasts.

---

[a] Revelation 19:10   [b] Mark 13:30

Interconnectedness

The New Testament Fulfils
the Old Testament Promises

To understand how the New Testament is a fulfilment of Old Testament promises, it is important to understand that Jesus' words recorded in the gospels are always rooted in Old Testament concepts in general and more specifically in the Torah. For the Torah lies at the heart of Jewish scriptures as it was the first scripture to be recognized as an authoritative document. [19]

As a Christian, we confess that the Word of God, that is the eternal Torah, has become incarnate, made flesh in Jesus Christ,[20] for we believe that Jesus is the end of the law and significantly, for this discussion, the *'telos'* of the Torah. [a] In fact the entire Torah points towards Christ.[b]

Equally important we need to understand how Jesus interpreted the Torah[21] because it is here over this point that the Pharisees and Sadducees argued so strongly against him. Jesus went much further than they did. For him, the Torah and the Tenach, that is, the entire Scripture together held out the promise or announcement of a coming Messiah.[c] [22] I believe that Jesus and the evangelists consider that the entire Tenach foreshadows what is to come.[d] [23] The facts of salvation as described in the Old Testament are described in such a way in the New Testament to serve as an example or an *'hupódeigma'*.[e]

Even after the coming of Christ, the Old Testament is still connected to the present for "everything that was written in the past was written to teach us."[f] In this same sense, the Feasts of the Lord foreshadow things to come.[g]

---

a Romans 10:4 ; b Galatians 3:24 c John 5:39; Luke 24 d Matthew 5:17, 21-48
c 1 Corinthians 10:1-11 f Romans 15:4 g Colossians 2:16,17

This aspect of foreshadowing can be tied to the idea of 'typology' (*'túpos'*) where people from the Old Testament can serve as prototypes or analogies for the New Testament.[24] For some writers, typology can be defined as "an analogous way of thinking and speaking, that draws attention to two or more realities (e.g. Adam and Christ), thus emphasising their interconnectedness."[25]

Double Reference or Fulfilment

The explanation of the meaning of texts (exegesis) or typological interpretation is based on historical events with a literal meaning rather than a literary interpretation of events based on allegories and metaphors.[26] When we use analogous ways of understanding the interconnectedness of past and present, Old Testament events foreshadow things to come. [a] [27] For example, in the Old Testament, a high priest can be understood to be a typological figure represented in the figure of the high priest Melchizedek[28] and the sacrifice of Isaac can be understood also as typological figure referring to Christ's sacrifice to come.[b]

Turning to the New Testament, a clear example of typology that has been 'fulfilled' can be found in the words, "For Christ, our Passover lamb, has been sacrificed."[c] This New Testament writer interprets the actual meaning from the Old Testament, and again from the actual events, he uses typological prophecy for the future.[29] Just as both the Torah and the Prophets point to John the Baptist in the New Testament so too the coming Kingdom of God is preached - and pointed to - from the time of Jesus onwards.[d] [30]

A typological exegesis in this instance seeks to understand what the New Testament actually means in Israel's salvation history. Thus this approach to typology is based on historical agreement between Old Testament as well as current events.[31] A typological approach can also be understood in the context of promise and fulfilment; God continues his work of salvation as a process in time. In other words, he performs new historical acts that consummate His previous ones in history.[e] [32]

This approach to typological exegesis matches the ordering of the Word of God in its promise, fulfilment, and consummation.[33] The criteria for interpreting these kinds of promises are clear and coherent: in addition to a literal interpretation, there is also a historical interpretation, which must agree with other promises—this is called the Law of Double Reference or Fulfilment.[34]

---

[a] Hebrews 10:1 [b] Hebrews 11:19 [c] 1 Corinthians 5:7 [d] Luke 16:16
[e] Ephesians 2:7

The Law of Double Fulfilment

B ased on my premises outlined above, when we examine the New Testament we can conclude that when we celebrate the facts of redemption in the present they offer us not only a reminder of what has happened
in history but also a perspective on what is yet to come. In the story of
salvation, history and future have been joined together; they are a single
'saving event' in two parts.[35] The Old Testament testifies about Christ for
the historical time of Christ[a] is the time that the prophets themselves
yearned for.[b] In that particular sense, the New Testament fulfils what is to
come.[c]

Both prophets and evangelists testify that God was revealed in Christ.[d]
Time and time again, the New Testament refers to Old Testament
prophecies with the important phrase "to fulfil what the Lord had said
through…".[e]
Time and time again, Jesus himself explains that the Scriptures apply to
Him [f] and that He has fulfilled the Old Testament precepts confirming the
truth of God's Old Testament actions in the present moment.[g][36] Jesus'
interpretation of the Old Testament promises, however, will be consummated in the future.[h][37] A future consummation of the coming Messiah is
always connected to the historical fulfilment of the New Testament message.[38,39]
A key question is this: Is this why Jesus took such care to recognize the
importance of Feasts during his lifetime in order that their highest purpose
will be fulfilled?[40]

---

[a] John 5:39 [b] Mark 13:16,17 [c] 1 Peter 1:10 [d] Hebrews 1:1
[e] Matthew 1:23; 2:25,17,23; 4:14 [f] Luke 4:21; Luke 24 [g] Hebrews 2:6
[h] Mark 1:14,15

The Importance of Feasts

A Key Question

We recognize the ongoing effect of God's past actions early on in the Old Testament as well as their ability to model for the present. God is going to free his nation step-by-step.[a] Like a true love affair, the on-going relationship between God and His people is a step-by-step process from engagement to a wedding celebration. Israel's sojourn in the desert wilderness is seen not only as a period of engagement between God and Israel, [b] but also is a preparatory period for Israel's return to God after a period of apostasy.[41] There in the wilderness foundations were laid to celebrate the Passover (*Pesach*) and the Feast of Weeks (*Shavuot*), but the celebration of the great feast, the Feast of Tabernacles (*Succoth*), would be delayed until His people had arrived in the Promised Land.

Certain questions may now come to mind. Do these examples show us that there is a certain order in the feasts? Could the idea of the feasts be a typology, a foreshadowing of the future? Does the Feast of Tabernacles, the great feast with all the Messianic expectations associated with it, have a typological basis in the Old Testament?[42] In this respect will the Old Testament be confirmed in the New Testament?[43] Can we find any New Testament reference to the Feast of Tabernacles, the great feast, at which time God comes to the 'tabernacle' among his people?[c]

We may assume that the Feast of Tabernacles is a window into the future, a glimpse of a future of living 'in tents' and that it expresses a deep-seated yearning for the Messiah, who will come to celebrate the final great feast.

---

[a] Exodus 1-15   [b] Hosea 2   [c] Revelation 21:3

Typological Implications

In Christian thought, typological interpretation has certain implications.[44] From the New Testament perspective, Church Fathers concur with this typological meaning.[45] We read that when Israel led out of Egypt like a child it is understood to be a typological reference to Christ.[a][46]

J. Danielou is one leading scholar who can be identified with this typological approach.[47] Daniélou argues that a line, a tradition of thought, can be drawn from Judaism to the Church Fathers. In other words, he ascertains that Jewish liturgy affected the symbols of the Church Fathers. To him, typology has a twofold interpretation. It is both explanatory and yet allusive. Explanation is commonplace but allusion remains unknown and so Daniélou moves into Christological and sacramental typology. Isaac's sacrifice is one example of Christological typology according to Danielou.[b][48] The crossing of the Red Sea which is an example of New Testament sacramental typology can be understood as a typology of the sacrament of baptism. [c]

Danielou's argument or proposition is that Christian sacraments find their roots or origins in Jewish liturgy.[49] Two other scholars, W.J. Barnard and P. van 't Riet, also link together Jewish liturgy with Christian sacraments, that is, the Seder liturgy and the sacrament of the Lord's Supper.[50]
O. Cullman also supports this proposition that the Biblical foreshadowing of Passover is found in the sacraments.[51]

For these scholars among others, God's acts of salvation revealed in the Old and New Testament apparently affect our liturgy.[52] A. Noordegraaf writes, "The use of Scripture in the NT has been determined by the salvation-historical / Christological testimony about the fulfilment in the last days, while, formally, Jewish exegetic rules are applied."[53]

---

[a] Matthew 2:15 [b] Hebrews 11:19 [c] 1 Corinthians 10

In following Noordegraaf's focus on such Jewish exegetical rules, presumably Old Testament evangelists used such exegetical rules that were formerly laid down in the Midrash.[54] In the Midrash, the narrative method is commonly used to interpret the Tenach. In turn, this typological interpretation contrasts with the rabbinical Midrash because historical events always form the foundation or basis when using typological interpretations.

In the Footsteps of the School of Antioch

Early Church scholars and thinkers were apparently aware of typological exegesis[55] as there were different schools in Alexandria and Antioch using different interpretative tools for different passages. On the one hand, early scholars such as Origen and Clement from the Alexandrian School favoured the allegorical method of exegesis although they were familiar with literal methods of interpretation. Through St. Augustine[56] in particular, the Western Church continued to follow in this allegorical tradition.

However, the School of Antioch favoured a more literal interpretation ascribing a typological meaning to Old Testament interpretation. For this school, there was no room for allegorical interpretation in the New Testament, and it is within this particular viewpoint that the Eastern Church[57] followed a literal interpretation of scripture.

Ancient Antioch

17

Typologies of Foretelling

In the earliest centuries of church history, church historians focused on Messianic expectation, that is, they understood or perceived that the Kingdom of God was mainly focused on foretelling.[58] Over time in the development of church history, other aspects of interpretation took centre stage while the emphasis on this particular dimension lessened.[59] In the New Testament Letter to the Hebrews[60] which cites the Old Testament as many as 35 times, we discover an orientation to the future, that is, a sense of a pilgrimage for God's people who as believers and pilgrims are now called to walk by faith.[a]

Jesus is a visible fulfilment of Old Testament promises, an image of future hope. Significantly this contrasting typology of past and future has now been refashioned into another contrasting typology of the visible and invisible.[61] Here we have a symbolic typology of the visible, that is, the visible image[62] which may have replaced first century expectations of the future with expectations of a heavenly image. Augustine (who believed that the Millennium Kingdom had already come in his lifetime) endorses this view of a heavenly image.

Christians in the west tend to think linearly, following Augustine; they start with the past then move along a straight line into the present, then towards the future.[63] Augustine expresses his sense of linear time in several of his books *Het onderwijzen van nieuwelingen*, and *The City of God,* for him the prophecies will come true — in time.[64]
Moreover he is specifically opposed to the Neoplatonic cyclical view of history.[65]

---

[a] Hebrews 2

Hebrew Old Testament Thought

Hebrew Old Testament thought focuses directly on the here-and-now[66] which differs with Greek thought expressed in the work of the Neoplatonists and Augustine for example. Standing in the centre of a circle as it were, the Hebrews drew a wide circle out from the centre of the here-and-now. This circle encompassed the past as well as the future together including the beginning as well as the end of time. The prophets stood rooted in the here-and-now enveloping the future in their thinking but always it was from their present position in the moment.[67]

Let us see what happens in New Testament thought based on this approach to time and history. Jesus comes in the fullness and centrality of time.[a] The particular typological view of time follows this model, that is, a concentric understanding of history.[68] Historical reliability is central in contrast with an allegorical sense of time, where hidden meanings are more important than literal reliability and interpretation.

According to the scholar W. Zuidema, the concept of 'time' in Israel was not an abstract idea but rather was a singularly empirical fact, a category of consciousness, which is why Israel was so aware of past events and history. The concept of 'simultaneity' expresses this idea so aptly.[69] Lived experience for Israel is communal as well as individual but always experienced in time.[70] Within the liturgical narrative of the Seder, for example, the 'first person is plural', that is, communal as well as individual so that each new generation can identify with its past as though it actually participated in the Exodus out of Egypt. One central purposes of commemoration of these feasts is to confirm God's acts in the present moment.[71] The collective consciousness represents everyone at all times and places.[72]

---

[a] Ephesians 1:10 ; Galatians 4:4

The Significance of the Sabbath

Collective consciousness and the experience of time as an historical fact have affected the development of modern Christian liturgy.[73] Judaism has structured a sense of time through the weekly Sabbath as well as through annual festivals.[74] The Sabbath for them is rooted in the created order of things.[75] In other words, counting the days leading up to the weekly Sabbath has to do with this created sense of orderly progression through time,[a] this sense of the end of a week coming to a close and to a day of rest.

According to the Book of Exodus, when we celebrate the Sabbath we are reminded that God is our Creator and humankind needs a day of rest, and equally important every human being draws their very life and breath from God.[b][76] Furthermore, the typology of the Sabbath is a model for the final day of rest or destiny with God.[c][77] This concept draws us back yet again to the New Testament as an order to Messianic Jews.[d][78] Jesus declares that He has 'come to give us rest' meaning that X.[e] The Apostle Paul writes about the Sabbath as a foreshadowing of future things and about Christ's interpretation of this foreshadowing.[f]

How does the Sabbath as a typology concerning time affect feasts? In the Old Testament Leviticus Chapter 23 tells us that the Sabbath was pre-eminent in its list of feasts. Seven days of the week follow one-by-one serving as a weekly pattern for the liturgical pattern of the week[79] that is built upon it. Is this a pattern for the order of the festivals beginning in the first month and concluding in the seventh?
Let's take a closer look to examine the pattern of the Christian liturgical week.

---

[a] Psalm 90:12 [b] Exodus 31:16,17 [c] Isaiah 66:23 ;Ezekiel 44:24
[d] Hebrews 4:9 [e] Matthew 11:28 [f] Colossians 2:16,17

The Pattern
The Christian Liturgical Week

Feasts are specific feasts of the Lord: this is the most important foundation for the argument that feasts have intrinsically built within them an element of foretelling, a hint of things to come. Ultimately it is God who has ordained the relationship between historical events in time because He is the Creator, the One who was, is, and is to come.[a] Out of the centre point of the present we can scan the past and look ahead to the future.

Hebrew thought imagines this sense of order in time: the present lies at the centre of the circle of time with other circles of time encircling the past and the future. In Christian thought as expressed in the New Testament God is understood as the God of the living, that is, the God of all humanity living now in the current moment of time.[b] The very name of God, JHWH, emphasizes the living moment in time, for God declares that 'I am Who I am',[c] that is the eternal now.

Similarly in the Old Testament, the 'God of Abraham, Isaac, and Jacob' declares that God is also the God of the past which is an experience of time distinct from the present. In the statement 'I will be who I will be' God also declares that even the future belongs to Him as well.

The Bible shows us how important time is in the biblical portrayal of the Son of God as well as God himself. In Galatians and Ephesians, we see that the Son of God came in the fullness of time,[d] and it is this *'pléroma',* this experience of time, that is the centre of time. Jesus says that He is the Alpha and the Omega which shows us that Jesus understands that He spans the beginning and the end of time.[e]

For a moment, let us look at how this sense of time is paralleled in the New Testament church. For example, in the Lord's Supper, we see how

---

[a] Revelation 1:4 [b] Matthew 22:32 [c] Exodus 3:14 [d] Galatians 4:4
Ephesians 1:10 [e] Revelation1:8, 21, 6, 22:13

the spotlight falls on the moment of celebration when X commands us that we should do this in remembrance of what Jesus did until He returns.[a] The New Testament connects together the notion of redemption, commemoration and foreshadowing. The New Testament also tells us that celebration of God's redemptive acts is a commemoration as well as a foreshadowing.

Let's digress for a moment – away from the discussion of this Old and New Testament pattern to discuss the institution and development of feasts as well as how feasts are actually celebrated.

First let's interpret what feasts really mean. The circles of time that encircle each historical feast show us its ongoing effect and future importance. This can only be discussed at the end of our study because the circles of the future are the outermost circles of the festivals — is it also perhaps their final conclusion?

Imagine the Feasts Unfolding

We have worked through a reasonable case for the argument that there is a prophetic or future-oriented dimension to God's feasts. Let's focus on what this future will be like and what it might be made of — our plan is to study all the Feasts of the Lord and to discover their prophetic significance. We will look at a series of related questions including structure, significance, fulfilment and consummation.

Will we discover a linear structure and significance – a line leading towards an ultimate climax of all feasts? Does that climax coincide with the Great Feast in the history of salvation when Christ returns and the coming age dawns? How will all prophetic promises ultimately be fulfilled and consummated? These are some of the questions we will address in The Feasts of the Lord, Chapter 3.

---

[a] 1 Corinthians 11

Chapter 3

The Feasts of the Lord

Our plan is to study all the Feasts of the Lord and to discover their prophetic significance. So let us begin with a focus on what this future will be like and what we could imagine what it will be made of. To achieve our goal we will examine a series of related questions dealing with structure, significance and consummation.

Let's begin with the feasts called '*Chagim*', which were appointed and established as set times by God. "These are the LORD's appointed feasts, the sacred assemblies you are to proclaim at their appointed times".[a] In the Torah, the festive days or feasts are mentioned seven times and in every instance the people are ordered to observe them[b] [80] particularly the three Great Feasts of Passover, the Feast of Weeks and the Feast of Tabernacles.

---

[a] Leviticus 23:4 [b] Exodus 12, 13; Exodus 23:12-19 ; Exodus 34:18-25
Leviticus 23 ; Numbers 28-29 ; Deuteronomy 16

3.1

The Feast Calendars: The Time of the Feasts

It is interesting to examine when the feasts actually took place as described in the Old Testament books of Exodus, Leviticus, Numbers, Deuteronomy and Ezekiel. To answer this issue we need to examine whether the actual order of festival times provide us with clues to the order of time itself. Will the structure of festive days reveal something important about their past and future?

The oldest festive calendars and the timing of the feasts are woven together with the movement of the sun and the moon. Various scriptural passages provide us with specific details of how the notion of time played an important part in the final decisions when feasts began. The actual times of the feasts, 'Mo'adim', were determined by the positions of the sun as well as the moon as they moved across the face of the earth.[a]
Interestingly the singular 'Mo'ed' means a certain time or place.[81]

These feasts were first mentioned in the Old Testament book of Exodus Chapters 23 and 34. In fact, the calendars of feasts are considered to be the oldest historical calendars that we have concerning the history of Old Testament feasts.[82] Both calendars in Chapters 23 and 24 mention the same three important feasts, the Feast of Unleavened Bread, the Feast of Harvest, and the Feast of Ingathering. Scholars assume that these liturgical calendars are linked to ancient agricultural ways of life.[83] Unfortunately liturgical calendars do tell us something important about how they celebrate these feasts but they do not tell us when these feasts should actually be held.

---

[a] Genesis 1: 14-16

The liturgical calendar for the Passover (*Pesach*) celebration refers to God's redemptive acts in redeeming his people out of bondage in Egypt. The four-day preparation[a] began with the choosing of a lamb in Aviv, [b][c] the first month of the year. Interestingly the word '*Pesach*' literally connotes something like the feast of sparingly passing[84] for the passage in Exodus 12:1-13 describes how God passes over his people. The word 'Pesach' is derived from the verb '*pasach*' meaning 'passing' or 'jumping over something'. This is perhaps why the feast is quite literally understood to mean 'the LORD's Passover'.

The Feast of Passover is intimately connected with the Feast of Unleavened Bread in Exodus 12:14-20. In other instances, these two feasts, the Feast of Passover and the Feast of Unleavened Bread, are regarded as only one feast,[d] not two. Different scholars have expressed different viewpoints to explain the relationship between these two feasts.

The first Passover together with the Feast of Unleavened Bread[85] was celebrated, presumably, only in the land of Canaan. In Exodus 12:29-51, the exodus of God's people begins under the cover of darkness while God keeps watch over them at night.

This annual feast signifies for every ensuing generation that they too must remember a night of keeping watch to honour the Lord. When we consider what lies at the heart of the feasts it is striking that this calendar mentioned in Exodus precisely specifies the periods in which the feasts are to be celebrated.[e]

The calendar contains obvious agricultural overtones and probably moments of agricultural celebration but also in addition the calendar was quite likely used during liturgical celebrations in the Temple. [In addition to the three feasts mentioned earlier, the calendar also gives instructions for two other feasts, that is, the Day of Trumpets and the Day of Atonement. This order demonstrates a strong affinity with other portions of scripture.][f]

---

[a] Exodus 12:1-13 [b] Exodus 12:2 [c] Exodus 13:4 [d] Exodus 23:15 [e] Leviticus 23 [f] Numbers 28-29

In Leviticus 23, the feast calendar tells us about the dates and precepts of each feast. Interestingly, the same rhetorical form of introduction is used for the five feasts in verses 1, 9, 23, 26 and 33, that is, "The LORD said to Moses". The fact that Leviticus 23 focuses on describing the Sabbath first is not in itself unusual.[a] According to the scholar J.E. Hartley,[86] there is an addition at the end namely that the Feast of Tabernacles is called 'a festival to the Lord' or 'the Lord's Feast'.[b] Hartley's annotation may be understood to deal with the position the Feast of Tabernacles was going to take among the feasts as a whole. The Feast of Tabernacles is referred to as 'The Festival' in other instances[c] so it seems more likely that the Feast of Tabernacles was regarded as the most important festival both as an institution and its place in history.

In Numbers Chapters 28 and 29, the feast calendar comments on the liturgical cycle of Leviticus 23 telling us at which feast which sacrifices should be made. These chapters of Scripture describe how the sacrifices were ordered, presumably as they were made after the Exile out of Egypt.[d] [87]
In Numbers 29, the Passover appears to have been surpassed by the Feast of Tabernacles in importance when we consider the number of sacrifices the feast involves. Moreover, the Feast of the New Moon has been included for some reason in the list of feasts.

The liturgical calendar described in Numbers Chapter 28-29 is important because it gives us an overview of the feasts themselves. According to scholars, the sacrifices described in Numbers Chapters 28-29 have become primarily individual offerings possibly pointing to a later historical development. Numbers Chapters 28-29 can be seen as an addition to Leviticus 23 and Deuteronomy 16.[88] Later developments probably made Passover a domestic celebration making offerings in the Temple no longer necessary or perhaps these precepts were kept alive from other previous Scriptural passages. This may be the reason why we find here an emphasis on the distinction between the Passover and the Feast of Unleavened Bread.

---

[a] Exodus 23 [b] Leviticus 23:33,41 [c] Numbers 29:12 ; Judges 21:19 ; Hosea 9:5
[d] 2 Kings 24:1

The liturgical calendar described in Deuteronomy 16 focuses only on the three great feasts[89] giving us more details about the dates and duration of the feasts in comparison with the calendars in Exodus Chapters 23 and 34. Yet again the Passover is given a central place as a pilgrim feast during the month of Aviv.[90] No mention is made, however, of The Feast of Unleavened Bread but we assume that it is part of the Passover.

The precepts found in Deuteronomy Chapter 16:1-15 mention the same three pilgrim feasts as does Exodus Chapters 23 and 34. This specific passage differs from the other two passages in that it refers to the Feast of Ingathering as '*Sukkoth*' the Feast of Tabernacles. The festive calendar found in Deuteronomy 16 states clearly that God will choose where the feasts are to be celebrated.[91]

Now we come to the last calendar, the one festival mentioned in Ezekiel Chapter 45, which refers to only two feasts, that is, the Passover and the Feast of Tabernacles, each feast lasting for seven days. Ezekiel 45:18-20 contains also precepts for two days of Atonement. We discover that Ezekiel 45 reveals a specific order and prophetic significance that is a future feast was to be held during the first month then another future feast was held during the seventh[92] but the Feast of Weeks is not mentioned. Which calendar gives us the correct ordering of time?

In terms of length, we discover that the shortest calendar is mentioned in Exodus Chapter 23:14-17 - "Three times a year you are to celebrate a festival to Me", a '*Chag*'. These three feasts are called *Matzot* (Unleavened Bread), *Qasir* (Harvest), and *Asif* (Ingathering) which was still held in the autumn at the 'end of the year'.

In comparison to Exodus 23:14-17, Exodus Chapter 34:18-23 mentions three feasts with the Ingathering held at the 'turn of the year'. The 'end of the year' mentioned in Exodus 23:16 and the 'turn of the year' mentioned in Exodus 34:22 are similar expressions meaning the same thing: they depend on the calendar being used.[93]

Civil and Religious Calendars

A civil calendar begins in the autumn while a religious calendar starts in the spring. The civil year always starts with 'the head of the year' Rosh Hashanah, which marks also the beginning of the Autumn Feasts. Significantly during the time of the Exodus, God revealed that the religious year was to begin with the Exodus for "This month is to be for you the first month".[a] In the Talmud, we read that the 1st Nisan is the beginning of the feasts and the 1st Tishri is the New Year Feast. [94]

To summarize we call the year beginning with Rosh Hashanah the start of the civil year and the year beginning with Passover the start of religious year. God made a new beginning, according to the Bible, when He instituted the religious year with Passover as the Feast of Redemption.[b]
Do these consecutive calendars show us a certain development, or do they supplemental each other?

People have tried to answer this particular question by saying that Exodus Chapter 23 and 34 uses the civil calendar while the religious calendar was not used until Leviticus 23. As early as Exodus Chapter 12:2, however, God indicates that the beginning of the feasts begins with the month of Aviv, the Month of Spring. Although Aviv is a Canaanite name, there is no question here of adapting the feast to the customs of surrounding nations. Only later do they call this month is called Nisan following the Babylonian order.[c] [95] If Leviticus 23 was written at a later date, why does this chapter not include the name of the Feast of Weeks?[96]

In Deuteronomy Chapter 16:1-7 we discover that the calendar begins with the religious order stating that the three feasts are *Matzot* (Unleavened Bread) in the month of Aviv, *Shavuot* (Feast of Weeks) for the harvest, and *Sukkoth* (Feast of Tabernacles) for the ingathering.

---

[a] Exodus 12:2 [b] Exodus 13 [c] Nehemiah 2:1

The list of feasts outlined in Numbers 28-29 also refers to an addition to the offerings to be made during the feasts mentioned in Leviticus 23.[97]

Deuteronomy 16.2, by comparison, does speak of the offerings to be made at the Feast of Passover. Numbers Chapter 28 distinguishes clearly the Feast of Passover from the Feast of Unleavened Bread yet in Ezekiel Chapter 45 these two separate feasts are considered as one.[98] For the time being, it appears that we cannot see any development in the calendars but instead let's look at the calendars in relationship to each other.

The Issue of Cultural Influences

Following the order of the feasts throughout the year we can examined the influence of the changes in season in agricultural life. Did God appoint these feasts directly or did Israel copy these feasts from Canaanite tradition? Was the final interpretation of the feasts influenced by the mingling of cultures together with their institutions such as the names of the feasts[100] for example?

Let us examine briefly the belief that cultural influences directly affected the final interpretation of feasts. Firstly, the Feast of Weeks is called the Feast of Harvest or the Day of First fruits of the wheat harvest. The Feast of Tabernacles is called also the Feast of Ingathering.[a] Sometimes, the calendar links together the Feast of Passover to the Feast of Unleavened Bread and because of these linkages the relationship between an agricultural way of life and the feasts is assumed. Furthermore there is the cultural fact of the offering of a one-year-old lamb which was practised by nomadic peoples in their homes.[100]

---

[a] Exodus 34:22

Other scholars differ: they assert that the eating of unleavened bread was directly ordained by God, that it was a practice Israel was specifically ordered to honour from the time of the Exodus. I believe that we can safely conclude that God instituted these feasts before the Israelites left Egypt.[a]

The Biblical scholar A. Cole argues that there were several interwoven influences on the development of the feasts, that the feasts were affected on the one hand by God's acts in history and on the other hand by agricultural life.[101] Feasts were not a single static phenomenon but rather underwent a dynamic development.

The feasts that came about in history such as the Feasts of Purim and Chanukah confirm this development.

Let's take a closer look.

The Three Great Feasts

The Feast of Unleavened Bread, the Feast of Harvest, and the Feast of Ingathering are the three great feasts that always occupy centre stage.[b] Other names for these three are Feast of Pesach or Passover, Feast of Weeks, and Feast of Tabernacles. In addition other festivals were known to have existed beyond these three great feasts, but we will restrict ourselves here to the three great feasts, or 'Chagim'. In Leviticus 23, the term 'Chag' is used only for the two seven-day feasts, i.e. the Feast of Unleavened Bread and the Feast of Tabernacles.[102] 'Chag' means 'festival with a religious purpose'. The etymology of the word is unclear, the meaning having been developed from 'round', via 'circular' to 'dance'. The OT 'Chag' means a festive gathering, usually assuming a pilgrimage to a central place.[103]

When did these three great feasts come to be regarded as pilgrim feasts? Was it perhaps when the people entered the Promised Land, or later?

---

[a] Exodus 12 [b] Exodus 12, 23, 24, 34

Year after year the Bible says that Elkanah went to the tabernacle in Shiloh[a] which presumably was on the occasion of the Feast of Tabernacles. If this is the case then the Feast of Tabernacles was already a pilgrim feast during the time of the Book of Judges. Generally scholars assume that the other two feasts were not regarded as pilgrim feasts until the construction of the Temple.[104]

We read, on several occasions, that the Feast of Unleavened Bread was a pilgrim feast celebrated in the Temple.[b] The calendars mentioned in Exodus Chapters 23 and 34 reveal that there was a central place of celebration for the Feast of Unleavened Bread, and that this feast, already celebrated at the time of Joshua, was directly connected with the Exodus. This feast was already celebrated with the eating of the first grain in the land of Canaan. It symbolizes the urgency about leaving Egypt as well as the eating of the first bread in the Promised Land.[c] This kind of interpretation leaves us with little room for Canaanite influences.

In the Feast of Weeks or the Feast of Harvest, we can see that there is an agricultural connection to the second name for this feast, that is, the Feast of Harvest. Yet importantly Israel has always connected the direct acts of God with this feast rather than with the changing agricultural seasons.[d]

The Feast of Weeks is an allusion to the 50 days after the Passover Feast when Passover was completed. Moreover, this feast is short lived, that is, it is celebrated for only one day which is why some scholars believe this feast has played a relatively unimportant role in Israel's history of salvation. For it was only after the Exile that the Feast of Weeks was explicitly associated with lawmaking on Mount Sinai.[e] [105] If we turn, however, to the actual date in Exodus Chapter 19:1 we discover that Exodus associates this particular feast with lawmaking so that we must conclude that the Feast of Weeks was important to Israel early in its history.

---

[a] 1 Samuel 1:3, 21   [b] Ezra 6; John 11:55-57; Matthew 20:18
[c] Joshua 5:11   [d] Leviticus 23; Numbers 28 ; Deuteronomy 16
[e] 2 Chronicles 15:10-14

Early in Israel's history the Feast of Tabernacles was a pilgrim feast because it is referred to as the festival to the Lord[a] or, as a festival (feast) to the Lord[b] or, simply just as 'the feast' or 'the festival'.[c]

The Feast of Tabernacles is the most exuberant feast of all. It is bound up with God's redeeming work in the journey through the desert.[d]

Agricultural life affects this feast because we read that its second name is called the Feast of Ingathering.[106] Many scholars think of the origins of this feast as a tent feast; the Tabernacle was also a tent and it was only in Canaan that the tent was replaced by a booth. However, neither the oldest parts of Scripture[e] nor the more recent passages,[f] offer us conclusive evidence whether the Feast of Tabernacles was originally a tent feast or not. A tent and a booth were even interchangeable concepts.[g] [107]

This festival has been a pilgrim feast throughout the entire history of Israel. Once every seven years during this feast,[h] the Covenant was renewed (according to the summary of the Law in the Book of Deuteronomy) which may be the reason why Solomon chose this feast for the dedication of his Temple[i] — even after the Exile Ezra read from the Torah during this feast.

Throughout Israel's history, we can see how the feasts develop. In the Torah, the feasts are still called 'the festivals or feasts *of the Lord*'.[j]
As we read the prophet Isaiah the Lord says 'the feasts *of his people*' have become a burden to Him,[k] because people's lives are not rooted in justice and righteousness.[108] History shows us that once in a while the people did not do what God asked them to do — in other words they rebelled and the prophet Isaiah had to call on the people to repent.[109]

---

[a] Leviticus 23:39; Judges 21:19; Hosea 9:5 [b] Leviticus 23:41; Numbers 29:12 [c]
1 Kings 8:2, 65; 12:32 ; Ezekiel 45:25; Nehemiah 8:14 ;
2 Chronicles 5:3;8:7; John 7:2 [d] Leviticus 23:42 ff [e] Exodus 23, 24
[f] 2 Chronicles 5; Ezekiel 45 [g] Hosea 12:10 [h] Deuteronomy 31:10-13
[i] 1 Kings 8:2 [j] Numbers 28:1 [k] Isaiah 1:14

In the New Testament, feasts are no longer called 'the feasts of the Lord', but 'the feasts of the Jews' or 'the Jewish feasts'.[a] Did the feasts degenerate into something for just one nation? In Zechariah Chapter 14 the promise remains, nevertheless, that sometime in the future the Feast will be celebrated by every nation.

We can recognize a certain pattern in the development of the feasts from their creation by God himself and His promise concerning them through their historical development to God's fulfilment at the end of history. The order in the pilgrim feasts and the Feast of Tabernacles as the 'Great Feast' gives us some understanding of the order and sense of time. Do the Feasts thus tell us something important about the course of history?

---

[a] John 2:13;5:1;6:4;11:55

3.2

The Torah Readings

How time is ordered according to festive days or festivals continually affects Israel's entire religious and social life.[110] The precepts and offerings for the feasts are not isolated events even the reading of the Torah is bound up with this sense of the ordering of time. For example, every seven years the Torah had to be read to the entire people after the year of debt release namely during the Feast of Tabernacles.[a] Early on in Israel's history the Torah was read in public but how did this tradition develop historically?

During the time of Ezra, the Torah was read aloud in its entirety beginning on the first day of the seventh month.[b] Moses and Ezra understand that there was a direct relationship between the Feast of Tabernacles and the reading of the Torah. What then is the meaning of the Torah for this feast? Ezra wanted the Torah to be read on the second and the fourth day of the week, the two market days and on the Sabbath. The early historian Josephus[111] writes that the reading of the Torah in public was an ancient tradition. The Mishnah tells us that the Torah was read on Monday, Thursday and Sunday (around the end of the second century).[112]

The New Testament also shows us that the Torah was read in public.[c] Actually it was the Babylonian Talmud[113] which was the first source to show us that the Torah was read aloud according to an approved cycle of successive readings. According to the Jerusalem Talmud, the Torah was divided into 153, 155 or 167 orders or 'sedarim' based on a three-year cycle in the land of Israel. Passover lies at the centre of this three-year cycle forming the heart of the Torah from Exodus to Numbers.

---

[a] Deuteronomy 31:10-13 [b] Nehemiah 8:1-8 [c] Cf 1 Timothy 4:13
1 Thessalonians 5:27 ; Colossians 4:16; Revelation 1:3

By comparison, the Babylonian Torah was divided into 54 orders following a one-year cycle which began on the Sabbath after the Feast of Tabernacles and ended on the last day of this feast, the Rejoicing of the Law, Simchat Torah.[114] This one-year cycle became widespread[115] especially from 600 AD to the present. Maimonides records in the twelfth century[116] that the one-year cycle was in general use but in addition the three-year cycle was still adhered to at certain times. The reading in the synagogue was completed together with a part from the Torah according to the Mishnah[117] along with a portion from the Prophets, the 'Haftarah' or 'completion'.

The origin of this usage is not certain but what is certain is that it was already known at the time of the writing of the New Testament.[a]
On festive days, a special passage, related to that feast, was read aloud.[b]
Concerning each feast, let us draw attention to certain related Torah passages.

The instructions recorded in the Talmud to spread the Old Testament readings evenly throughout the year provide us with circumstantial evidence. The Talmud, however, can give us some insights into the way in which Jewish tradition viewed the relationship between the order of the Tenach, the liturgy, and the ordering of the year.

The question remains: whether the liturgy of Israel has eschatological significance, and if so, in what ways?

By itself, the entire Old Testament is a criterion for Christians regardless of orders and liturgical readings. Both Moses and Ezra instructed the people to read the entire Torah every seventh year at the time of the Feast of Tabernacles.[f] Apparently there is a relationship between this Feast and the Torah. The Feast of Tabernacles is also called the Feast of the Open Book.[118] It seems likely that this relationship has affected the other feasts as well.

---

[a] Luke 4:17 ; Acts 13:15; 15:21   [b] Numbers 28:16-29;39

Let us examine the importance of the Torah readings for the feasts and for the Feast of Tabernacles in particular.

One reason why the Scripture readings are important is the idea that there is a relationship between the Feasts of the Lord and God's Revelation. Do the feasts constitute the framework within which Jesus' words and acts were written down in the Gospel of St. John? One can arrange the Gospel of St. John as follows: first the prologue,[a] then Jesus' appearance in public,[b] finally His death and resurrection.[c] [119] The central part in the Gospel of St. John, i.e. Jesus' public appearance, begins on the third day at a wedding.[d]

Is the purpose of Jesus' appearance to refer to His wedding, that is, the wedding of the Lamb?[e] To Jewish onlookers in Jesus' day, this third day refers to the prophet Hosea, who said that God will restore Israel and to the sign of Jonah.[f]
The purification of the Temple then takes place around Passover.[g] Jesus goes up to Jerusalem for a feast.[h] Twice Jesus heals a person on the Sabbath. The feeding of the five thousand is near the Feast of Unleavened Bread.[i] Then Jesus says that He is the Bread of Life.[j]

---

[a] Deuteronomy 31:11 ; Nehemiah 8 [b] John 1:1-18
[c] John 1:19-12:50 [d] John 13:1-23:25 [e] John 2:1 [f] Revelation 19:7
[g] Hosea 6:2 [h] John 2:13 [i] John 5:1 [j] John 6:4

The Life of Jesus and the Celebration of Feasts

The Feast of Tabernacles provides the backdrop for John Chapter 7 and 8 where Jesus says that He is the Light of the World.[a] Jesus confirms his words by healing a man who was born blind.[b] And Jesus' statement that He is the good Shepherd is made on this feast.[c]
The Feast of Hanukkah is the backdrop for John Chapter 12, where Jesus confirms that He is the Son of God.[d] The climax of the Gospel of St. John, when Jesus' performs His most significant deeds, takes place against the background of the Spring Feasts. John 12 deals with Jesus entering Jerusalem just before the Passover Feast. John Chapter 13:1 is just before Passover as well.

This is followed by the events around Passover with the death of Jesus. The resurrection takes place on the Day of Firstfruits.[e] The Gospel of John ends with the events that take place a few days after the Resurrection. The structure of the Gospel of John clearly places Jesus' words within the context of the Feasts. Obviously, the most important actions of Jesus in the Gospel of John are set around Passover.

Subsequently, the book of Acts begins where the Gospel of John has left off, i.e. with a description of the Ascension and then Pentecost. Once again, the Feasts provide the backdrop.
Even the last book of the Bible clearly includes the Feasts. Revelation is structured around the Feast of Tabernacles – the Feast of Tabernacles also being the Feast of the Open Book, or the Revelation of God's plan of salvation.[f]

Why are God's Feasts so important that even his own acts of salvation coincide with them? Does the New Testament follow the order of the feasts? Let's look in the next chapter at the possible relationships.

---

[a] John 8:12 [b] John 9 [c] John 10:11 [d] John 12:37 [e] John 20
[f] Revelation 4-5

Chapter 4

The Spring Feasts

God has ordained a total of seven feasts, a plenitude of festive days, to be celebrated throughout the year.

The **Spring Feasts** comprise four events: Passover, Unleavened Bread, Firstfruits, and Weeks. The first three take place in the same period (early spring), while the Feast of Weeks, *Shavuot*, is celebrated fifty days later, and rounds off the Spring Feasts.

There are three **Autumn Feasts** (see Chapter 5): the New Year Feast, the Day of Atonement, and the Feast of Tabernacles.

As we have seen, three of the Spring Feasts take place in the first month of the religious year. At the time of the Exodus out of Egypt God declared that the religious year would begin with this exodus, "This month is to be for you the first month".[a] The question we have to ask ourselves is, "If the feasts begin in the first month, will the climax then be at the end of the year or halfway through the year?"

Let's take a look at the relation between Spring Feasts and Autumn Feasts. We'll assume that the Sabbath, as a typology of time, indicates a parallel between the cycle of a week and that of a year. Just as the week begins on the first day and is completed on the seventh day (the Sabbath), the Spring Feasts begin in the first month, and culminate in the Autumn Feasts, which are celebrated in the seventh month.

---

[a] Exodus 12:2

4.1

The Feast of Passover (*Pesach*)

Passover is an extensive feast. From a historical point of view, Passover represents the transition from bondage to redemption, freedom, in the Exodus. As the first Spring Feast, Passover also marks the transition from winter to summer. Many Scriptural passages in the OT[a] and NT[b] refer to the Passover Feast.

The OT tells us of various Passover celebrations. The first Passover Feast was the historical Exodus out of Egypt, at the beginning of the Israelites' journey through the wilderness to the Land of Promise.[c]

The second Feast of Passover was celebrated in the wilderness, at the construction of the Tent of Meeting, the Tabernacle.[d] At the end of the wilderness journey, a Feast of Passover was celebrated under Joshua in the first month, as the Israelites entered the Promised Land.[e] King Hezekiah held a Feast of Passover in the second month.[f] And there was a great celebration of the Feast of Passover during the reign of King Josiah.[g]
During the Exile, Ezekiel saw a vision of a future Feast of Passover, without the Passover Lamb.[h] After the Exile, the Feast of Passover was restored under Ezra.[i]

After the destruction of the Temple, lambs had to be offered, and the Feast of Passover chiefly took place in the homes. This domestic celebration culminated in a Seder meal. We see here how religious life continually affected the development of the liturgy concerning the festivals.

---

[a] Exodus 12:1-13; 21-29; Leviticus 23:4,5; Numbers 28:16; 33:3
Deuteronomy 16:1-8 [b] Matthew 26:1,2; 17-75; 27:1-66 ; Mark 14-15
Luke 22-23 ; John 18-19 ; Hebrews 11:28 [c] Exodus 12
[d] Numbers 9:15 [e] Joshua 5:10,11 [f] 2 Chronicles 30 ; Numbers 9:6-14
[g] 2 Kings 23:21-23; 2 Chronicles 35:18,19 [h] Ezekiel 45:21 [i] Ezra 6:19

People are not allowed to have a Seder meal before the evening falls. At a Seder meal, four cups of wine are drunk to mark the four words of redemption: Exodus, Salvation, Redemption, and Acceptance.[a] In doing so, the four cups are mentioned: *Kaddesh*, (Blessing); *Maggid*, (Wrath); *Ge'ula*, (Salvation) and *Hallel*, (Praise).

The Seder is concluded with the singing of the *Hallel*.[b] [120] Sometimes a fifth cup is present, whose meaning has to do with bringing to the land.[c] This last cup, which is not drunk, is called Elijah's cup.[121] It is a sign that the redemption from Egypt is just a foreshadowing of Messianic salvation and consequently has a foretelling nature. The fifth cup and the wish traditionally voiced at the end of the Seder – to celebrate the feast in Jerusalem next year – support this Messianic line of salvation. The redemption out of Egypt is here a foretaste of Messianic salvation. Many rabbis believe the Messiah's herald will come during a Passover night.[d]

Passover shows that next to being a Liberator and a Redeemer, God is also a Bridegroom. Before redeeming his people from Egypt, God told Moses about his plans to marry his people. God is the one who accepts his people.[e] This acceptance, '*lakach*', is an expression for 'contracting a marriage'. God collects his Bride from Egypt to marry her, and to enter into a covenant with her at Mount Sinai. The Torah is the marriage contract at the closing of the Covenant.[122] The journey through the desert is like a bridal period.[f]

Was this journey meant to teach the bride to rejoice in the Law, on her way to the Promised Land and the Kingdom of God?[123] Before the journey through the desert begins, the scroll of the Song of Solomon is read during Passover feasts, as a sign of God's ardent love for his people.

The first Passover Feast was celebrated even before the actual redemption from Egypt. This suggests that Passover is and continues to be a festival of faith. Those celebrating it remember the Exodus out of Egypt, but also look forward to the ultimate Messianic salvation. In celebrating Passover,

---

[a] Exodus 6:6,7 [b] Psalm 113-118 [c] Exodus 6:7 [d] Haggai 2:6
[e] Exodus 6:2-9 [f] Jeremiah 2:2

looking to the future is always bound up with remembering and commemorating history. Once again, we see the present at the centre of things, with a circle reaching out to the past and the future.

Passover is the first major pilgrim feast for the people – a feast to look forward to. We encounter the same idea in the Torah readings. As early as five weeks before Passover, people are prepared for it by Scripture readings. The reading for the fifth Sabbath, *Shabat HaGadol*, deals with keeping the Sabbath[a] and with Elijah being the Messiah's herald,[b] Elijah who will be sent before the Great Day of the Eternal One. In this way, the Scripture readings highlight the Passover's prophetic dimension.

In the NT, the relations between Pesach and Yeshua are virtually unlimited.[c] Three Gospel authors (Matthew, Mark, and Luke) describe the last Supper as a Seder meal, the beginning of Passover.[124] Matthew binds up Passover with Jesus' crucifixion as the Son of Man.[d] [125, 126]
Both Matthew and Mark indicate the fulfilment of God's plan and the Scriptures through Jesus' death.[e] [127] In Luke's Gospel the connection with the future is more emphatic[f] than any cultic connection.[g] [128]

The Gospel according to John quotes Jesus' farewell speech[h] during the Passover meal.[129] This Gospel supports the concept that the Seder meal is also the Messiah's Passover meal by emphasizing that the Messiah is the Paschal Lamb.[130] Right at the start of the Gospel of John, John the Baptist introduces the Paschal Lamb, Jesus, by saying, "Look, the Lamb of God, who takes away the sin of the world!"[i]

This Paschal Lamb was announced as early as Isaiah 53.[131] What's new is that Jesus is this Lamb and that His death will bring about atonement for the sins of the world..[j] [132]

---

[a] Exodus 20 [b] Malachi 3:4-4:6 [c] Matthew 26-2; Mark 14-15;
Luke 22-23; John 13-19; Hebrews 11:28 [d] Matthew 26:1,2
[e] Matthew 26 ; Mark 14:18-21 [f] Luke 22 ;Jeremiah 31:31-34
[g] Exodus 24:8 [h] John 14-16 [i] John 1:29 [j] 1 Corinthians 5:7

In Jesus' days, the Paschal Lamb was chosen by the high priest on the 10th Nisan, at a location outside Jerusalem. A priest would take this lamb inside the city, and the people would sing Psalm 118, closing with the words, "Blessed is He who comes in the name of the LORD."

Jesus Himself prophesied the future fall of Jerusalem and the time when at long last permanent peace would come, "until you say, 'Blessed is he who comes'." The lamb was taken to the temple to be tested by everybody.

Jesus identified himself with the sacrificial lamb.[a] Thus we may assume that He entered Jerusalem right behind the traditional procession on the 10th Nisan, Palm Sunday, riding a donkey, an animal usually ridden by a king. It is revealing that at that moment even the people saw in Him the Messiah, the fulfilment of the prophetic expectation.[b] Apparently, now that they saw this OT ritual fulfilled, it made them think of the Messiah. The people wanted Him to take possession of the throne of David and free the people from Roman occupation.

Jesus did fulfil this latter expectation, though only partially, at His first coming. First, He went out to purify the Temple so the Feast of Unleavened Bread could be celebrated in the way God wanted. The rulers resented him for these actions. Jesus then quoted Psalm 8, saying that God has ordained praise even from children. Thus Jesus took a Messianic Psalm and applied it to Himself.

Psalm 8 starts off and finishes with praising God. The central section deals with man who – despite everything – is brought to glory through God. Elsewhere in the NT, Psalm 8 is also linked to Jesus.[c] So we see a Messianic Psalm from the OT being made relevant through Jesus.

Psalm 8 thus received its first fulfilment in Jesus. Because of it we keep looking forward to a final fulfilment in the days of the Messiah, when we shall reign and rule with Him over creation. Palm Sunday is a foreshadowing of the final fulfilment and consummation at the great feast.[133]

Once again, we see a familiar order: Promise, Fulfilment, Consummation. In identifying himself with the Passover Lamb, Jesus also had to meet all

---

[a] John 12:9-19 [b] Matthew 21:9 [c] Hebrews 2

its requirements. For it is not the **perfect** lamb that brings reconciliation, but the **slaughtered perfect** lamb. The lamb had to be slaughtered on the evening of the 14th Nisan in the presence of the entire nation. Likewise, many people were present at Jesus' crucifixion: the rulers of the nation, the inhabitants of Jerusalem, and the visitors to the Passover Feast. That Jesus exclaimed, "It is finished," has major significance in that it closes off something.[a] The high priest was accustomed to speaking these words at Passover, after the evening sacrifice, as a sign that the sacrifice had been accepted and the sins forgiven. Likewise, Jesus had to cry out these words, as a sign of real closure and definite salvation.

When celebrating the Lord's Supper, we, too, are celebrating a feast of remembrance as well as expressing a yearning for the future days of the Messiah, according to 1 Corinthians 11:26. We will celebrate the Lord's Supper until His return.

This prophetic element in Jesus' sacrifice, as the Passover Lamb, indicates that for Christians the feast is a sign of hope and thus has a foretelling nature. This foretelling nature is already expressed before Passover on Palm Sunday, when we say, "Hosanna, Blessed is he who comes."[b]

We've seen now that Passover has everything to do with redemption.[c] The redemption is threefold: redemption from slavery, redemption from Egypt, and being set apart for service to God. Passover is a night of vigil, in which people look forward to being delivered from night to day.
After the people had passed through the Reed Sea, the Feast of Firstfruits began. However, they were allowed to celebrate this Feast of Firstfruits for the first time only in the Promised Land, forty years later. Yet, already at the Exodus, God ordered the Israelites to celebrate it; in this way, God's order evokes a yearning for the Promised Land.

---

[a] John 19:30   [b] Matthew 21   [c] Exodus 11-13

4.2

The Feast of Unleavened Bread (*Matzot*)

The Feast of Unleavened Bread, or '*Chag HaMatzah*', has become the most central feast around Passover, because it lasts for seven days.[a] Pesach is only one day, but is directly followed by the seven-day Feast of Unleavened Bread.

The word '*Chag*' is used only for seven-day feasts, such as the Feast of Unleavened Bread and the Feast of Tabernacles. The Feast of Unleavened Bread frequently occurs in the OT[b] and the NT.[c]

The Feast of Unleavened Bread starts on the night of the 14th Nisan and lasts till the 21st Nisan. According to Leviticus 23, it starts on the 15th Nisan, presumably because of the Hebrew counting from evening to evening: from the night of the 14th Nisan, it is already the 15th Nisan. The feast lasts for seven days, seven being a symbol of fullness.[d]

Like every other feast, it starts with a Sabbath, so that there is a normal Sabbath in every Passover week. During this feast, people eat unleavened bread for seven days. Unleavened bread, '*Matzot*', refers in particular to separation and dedication to the Lord. Because of the Exodus, the Israelites had to break completely from all ordinary Egyptian food.

Unleavened bread was used in Israel when priests were consecrated.[e] It was also used at the vow of a Nazirite,[f] in grain (meal) offerings, and in fellowship (peace) offerings as food for the priests.[g]

---

[a] Exodus 23:14-15 [b] Exodus 12:8; 15-20; 31-39; 13:3-10
Deuteronomy 16:1-8; Numbers 28:17-25; Leviticus 23:6-8
[c] Matthew 26:17-19 ; Mark 14:12-21; Luke 22:1-2; 1 Corinthians 5:6-8
[d] Exodus 12:15-19 [e] Leviticus 8:2,26; Exodus 29:2,23
[f] Numbers 6:1-12   [g] Leviticus 2:4-5; 6:14-18; 7:11-13

Jesus celebrated this Feast of Unleavened Bread in the NT.[134] He purified the Temple, as a preparation for Passover and the Feast of Unleavened Bread.[a] After the purification, Jesus could celebrate the feast in the way God wanted.[b]

Not only did Jesus celebrate the Feast of Unleavened Bread, He himself was the Living Bread come down from heaven, the manna, the unleavened bread. Paul wrote, "For Christ, our Passover Lamb, has been sacrificed. Therefore let us keep the Festival with bread without yeast, the bread of sincerity and truth."[c] [135]

Keeping the feast with bread without yeast refers to the sacrament of the Lord's Supper.[136] This sacrament can only be celebrated in holiness and truth, once the old yeast has been removed from our lives.[d]

[a] John 2:12; Mark 11:15 [b] Isaiah 1:144 ff [c] 1 Corinthians 5:7-8
[d] 1 Corinthians 11:23-34

4.3

The Feast of Firstfruits (*Bikkurim*)

The Feast of Firstfruits, *Bikkurim* (sometimes called *Yom habikkurim*), completes the Feasts of Passover and Unleavened Bread. This Feast of Firstfruits was not celebrated until the Israelites had entered the Promised Land, forty years after the Exodus.[a]

Israel was already familiar with the concept of Firstfruits, *'Begor'*.[137] All the first-born offspring of man and animal were holy before the Lord.[b] The first-born took centre stage at Passover. Here we are dealing with the firstfruits of the harvest, *'Bikkurim'*, which are holy, belong to the Lord, and are presented to Him.[c] During the journey through the desert, the Israelites were fed with manna, unleavened bread from heaven. However, they were not allowed to celebrate the feast until they had reached the Promised Land.[d]

The priest was to wave a sheaf of the first grain of the land, wheat and barley, before the countenance of the Lord, on the day following the Sabbath. Only after the first sheaf had been offered to God, were the Israelites allowed to eat the new grain. This sheaf heralds the further harvest.

Both the early harvest of the Feast of Firstfruits (the barley harvest), and the harvest of the Feast of Weeks (the wheat harvest) announce the late, great harvest to take place at the Feast of Tabernacles. The fact that God in His faithfulness has provided the early harvest, gives hope for an abundant late harvest.[138] Celebrating the early harvest by thanking God strengthens our faith in God for adding and providing all that is needed in the future.

---

[a] Leviticus 23:9-14; 1 Corinthians 15:20-23 [b] Exodus 13:2
[c] Deuteronomy 26:1-11; 18:3-5; Leviticus 19:23-25; Nehemiah 10:34-39
[d] Joshua 5:10-12

Starting from the day of the Feast of Firstfruits, Israel had to carry out the Omer count.[139] There are fifty days between the Feast of Firstfruits and the Feast of Weeks, *Shavuot*.[a] Just as the Firstfruits contain a promise of what is to come, the Omer counting is a time of expectation. People were not only looking forward to the early harvest, but also to the day of redemption. The number fifty symbolizes freedom and redemption.[b]

That is why the Year of Jubilee, as the year of redemption and freedom, was celebrated every fifty years.[c] In counting the Omer, the fifty days, Psalm 67 is sometimes quoted, because it consists of seven verses and 49 words.

There are two methods for the Omer counting. The Sadducean method starts from the day after the Sabbath (the weekly Sabbath); this day is taken as the beginning of the Omer counting and the Feast of Firstfruits. Current counting is based on the rabbinical method which starts from the day after *Pesach* (also a Sabbath) as the beginning of the Omer counting and of the Feast of Firstfruits.

In the NT, Christ is both Lord of the harvest and firstfruit[d] The Feast of Firstfruits, on the 17th Nisan, coincides with the resurrection of Christ, as the Firstborn from the dead. This Feast of Firstfruits specifically indicates Christ's sinlessness, in his sacrifice to God. In these offerings, Christ is present at Passover as a lamb (a sign of His death). At the Feast of Firstfruits He is present as a sheaf of Firstfruits (a sign of His resurrection).

---

[a] Leviticus 23:15 [b] Genesis 6:15; 1 Kings 18:4; 2 Kings 2:7;
Leviticus 27:1-5; Mark 6:40; Luke 9:14 [c] Leviticus 25:8-17
[d] 1 Corinthians 15:20-23

4.4

The Feast of Weeks (*Shavuot*)

The Feast of Weeks is the final feast of the Spring Feasts, fifty days after Passover.[a] In the NT we come across the Feast of Weeks as Pentecost.[b] Did God have this Feast of Weeks in mind when He told Moses that the Pharaoh had to let the Israelites go in order to have a festival for Him in the desert?[c] The rabbis also called the Feast of Weeks: '*Atzeret*' of Pesach.[140] '*Atzeret*' means 'closing' or 'anticipation'.

It is only in the Talmud that we find the first mention of the Feast of Weeks coinciding with the making of the Covenant at Mount Sinai.[141] Hence the rabbis call the Feast of Weeks '*Zeman Matan Torateynu*', because it was only at Mount Sinai that the Israelites received, so to speak, a heart. Thanks to this covenant, the nation has preserved its identity for centuries, even in times of oppression and exile. Just as Passover and *Shavuot* belong together, the Jewish nationality and identity are interwoven. The nation was called to be God's treasured possession out of all nations[d] and to be a kingdom of priests and a holy nation.[e]

The Ten Words can be regarded as a marriage certificate between God and the people. And God keeps the secret of His Covenant, the secret of His marriage with Israel.[142] According to the prophet Isaiah, God is the husband of his nation and He is called the God of all the earth.[f] Is it for this reason that the world will be aware of God's bond of marriage with Israel?[g] The Covenant of Mount Sinai still holds promise for the Covenant that will be written on their hearts.[h]

---

[a] Exodus 19-20; Deuteronomy16:9-12 ; Exodus 23:16-17;
Leviticus 23:15-21; Numbers 28:26-31;[b] Acts 2; 2 Corinthians 3-4;
Hebrews 8 [c] Exodus 5:1; 10:9 [d] Exodus 19:5 [e] Exodus 19:6
[f] Isaiah 54:5 [g] Isaiah 55:5 [h] Jeremiah 31:33

In addition to the Torah readings, the feasts also include a Prophet reading (*Haftarah* reading). At the Feast of Weeks, the *Haftarah* reading is from Ezekiel 1, the vision of the glory of the LORD. It is clear that the promises of Jeremiah 31 and Ezekiel 1 give the Feast of Weeks a prophetic dimension. Ruth is the feast scroll for the Feast of Weeks or *Shavuot*. [143]

Ruth is the perfect example of a person who has joined God's nation, out of love. Like Abraham, Ruth left her country of birth and her father's household[a] – to go to an unknown country, but in doing so she felt God leading her. Ruth has become an example for all people struggling for change.
The book of Ruth also shows God's care for poor people and widows. By Boaz' levirate marriage with Ruth, people experience the Joy of the Law. But even more importantly, this book tells us that Gentiles may become part of the nation of Israel through the Kinsman - Redeemer, the *Go'el*.
In God's prophetic promises, Israel learns that the Gentiles will also become part of God's nation, under the dominion of the Messiah.[b]
The Feast of Weeks is the beginning of this prophetic destination.

[a] Genesis 12:1 [b] Zechariah 14:9; Ezekiel 38,39

4.5

The Prophetic Significance
of the Spring Feasts

Let's have a look at the prophetic significance of the Spring Feasts. The three Feasts outline, so to speak, a programme for the nation. Israel's physical redemption starts at Passover, and takes place in stages. Firstly, God is the One Who leads out; He leads his people out of their worst sufferings in Egypt. Secondly, God is the Liberator; He liberates his people from slavery. Thirdly, God is the Redeemer; He redeems a blood relative, and, finally, God is the Bridegroom of his people; He accepts them as a nation.

God has collected his Bride from Egypt in order to contract a marriage with her at Mount Sinai. The Torah is the contract of marriage for the Covenant made between God and his nation. The journey through the desert can be compared with a bridal period: God is alone with his people.[a] On their way to the Promised Land and the Kingdom of God, the Israelites learned the Joy of the Law. Their future – i.e. that they would one day take possession of the Promised Land – was foreshadowed by the Passover Feast. And even though the Israelites now hold the land, there is still the prophetic Passover that will be celebrated during that Kingdom of God.[b] Then a Passover lamb will no longer be required to atone for sin – just unleavened bread as a token of sinlessness.

A fascinating question is whether the staged redemption at Passover is a model for the Messiah's second coming. Will that coming also take place in stages?
We have seen that already on the 10th Nisan, Palm Sunday, the prophetic promise was partially fulfilled with Jesus entering Jerusalem.

---

[a] Jeremiah 2:2 [b] Ezekiel 45

The people sang, "Hosanna, blessed is He who comes." The definite ful-filment did not come about at Pesach. Therefore, we may expect a future fulfilment or consummation of Passover.

Directly following Passover, the Feast of Unleavened Bread is celebrated. This seven-day event especially symbolizes separation from the past. It speaks about sanctification, being set apart. The NT indicates its impor-tance as well, "The old has gone, the new has come!"[a]

We find a second prophetic meaning in the unleavened bread, the '*matzot*': being fed with the hidden manna, with God's Word from heaven.[b]

At the end of the Passover week, on the seventh day of the Feast of Unleavened Bread, the people went through the Reed Sea.[144] The closing of this feast, '*Shevi'ih Shel*', indicates that the '*matzot*' has an end as the 'bread of affliction' and that a real physical redemption had come about through the waters of the Reed Sea. After the Israelites had left Egypt and gone through the Reed Sea, Moses sang his first song.[145]

Actually it's the first song of the *Tenach*,[c] with Miriam and the entire na-tion taking over. In it, the waters form the primal image of the powers of chaos, from which we need to be redeemed. The song can be regarded as a summary of the history of salvation, since it celebrates creation – a crea-tion that through redemption will lead to the Kingdom of God.[d]

In the sacrifice to God, the Feast of Firstfruits refers to Christ's sinless-ness. Christ is present here as the sheaf of Firstfruits, the sign of his resur-rection. Because the sheaf of Firstfruits had to be waved in God's house before his countenance, it also symbolizes Christ's ascension to be waved, as it were, before God's countenance in heaven. The sheaf of Firstfruits is distinguished from the harvest of Firstfruits.[e] The sheaf heralds the spring harvest, *Shavuot*.

On the 50th day of the Omer counting (starting from the Feast of Firstfruits), *Shavuot* or the Feast of Weeks takes place.[f] Despite its name, the Feast of Weeks lasts only for one day and forms the closing of the Spring Feasts. The barley offering of the spring harvest on this day is a

---

a 2 Corinthians 5:17 b Revelation 2:17 c Exodus 15:1-19
d see Revelation 15:3 e Exodus 23:16 f Leviticus 23:15

Firstfruit for the Lord.[a] The Feast of Weeks therefore is the feast of the first or early harvest. The Firstfruits speak of the rest that is still to come, at the great harvest.[b]

The parallel with the NT Feast of Weeks, or Pentecost, is remarkable. Here, first 3,000 and later 5,000 people were added to the church, as an early harvest.[c] The barley harvest at the Feast of Firstfruits and the wheat harvest at the Feast of Weeks are both precursors of the ultimate harvest, at the Feast of Tabernacles, the Harvest Feast at the end of the year.[d] As to the future fulfilment of this Feast of Firstfruits, we read in the last book of the Bible – Revelation – about the 144,000 who were offered as firstfruits to God and the Lamb, as the beginning of a great harvest.[e]

What then is the great Harvest Feast?[f]

Shavuot, the Feast of Pentecost, is regarded as the closing of *Pesach*, fifty days later. The church father Athanasius saw the closing of Passover at Shavuot as the Great Day of the Lord.[146] These fifty days are 7 x 7 + 1 day. The unity of seven days, or seven years, is a Biblical fact. But to complete the closing, to round off the Omer counting, an extra day is needed, a 50th day.

Is this extra day, this eighth day, an image of the future? What is the significance of the order of time? To God, the sanctity of time is of major importance, more than the sanctity of place. God has ordered time in a certain pattern: the week, with six days for creation and the seventh day for rest. After God's example, man may work six days and rest on the seventh day, the Sabbath.

In the Bible, the number seven indicates completeness, fullness. We see this 'seven' pattern recurring in the Feasts. But apparently, we are also dealing with an omission here. Even 7 x 7 is not sufficient for perfection. After 7 x 7 days, an extra day is needed to round off the Omer counting.

The years follow the same pattern. After six years, the seventh year is a

---

[a] Leviticus 23:17 [b] Hebrews 12:23 [c] Acts 4:4; 5:14
[d] Matthew 13:30 ; Mark 4:29; Revelation 14:15 [e] Revelation 14:4
[f] Matthew 13:36-43

Sabbath year in which slaves are released to regain their dignity. And after 7 x 7 years there is an extra Year of Jubilee, in which land is returned to its original owners, so that the new generation can make a new start.[a]
Apparently, after 7 x 7 days or years, something must be added to reach completion. This may have something to do with the eighth day or the eighth year.

Significantly, the eighth day is also the first day of a new week, a new year, and a new order/ -creation.[147] After the seven days, during which Aaron and his sons were ordained priests, their first ministry to God began on the eighth day.[b] This eighth day exceeds, so to speak, our perspective and our order of time. It tells us something about another side, God's side, a new beginning: the number 8 is the sign of the Messiah coming towards us from the other side, God's side, to perfect our situation.

The Year of Jubilee, as the 50th year, is a prelude to that new creation. Having read Isaiah 61 in the synagogue at Nazareth, Jesus called this Year of Jubilee the beginning of a new order. The usual readings accentuate the yearning for a new age, the coming century, 'Olam Haba'.[c]

We know God keeps watch over time. He will accomplish His redemptive work at his appointed time. Jesus came in the fullness of time.[d] And in order to receive God's Spirit, the disciples had to wait until the time of Pentecost had fully come.[e]
We have seen that the Feast of Weeks, *Shavuot*, is the closing of the Spring Feasts, but it cannot yet be the closing of all Feasts. Let's take a closer look at the Autumn Feasts in the next chapter, and see what these Feasts tell us about God's order of time.

---

[a] Leviticus 25:8 [b] Leviticus 9:1 [c] Jeremiah 31; Ezekiel 1
[d] Galatians 4:4 [e] Acts 2:1

Chapter 5

The Autumn Feasts

Just like the Spring Feasts, the Autumn Feasts are a combination of feasts. The well-known passage from Leviticus 23 indicates that all Autumn Feasts are celebrated in the seventh month and that there are three of them, i.e.,

- The Day of Trumpets on the 1st day
- The Day of Atonement on the 10th day
- The Feast of Tabernacles from the 15th to the 21st day.[a]

Let's take a closer look at the relation between these Autumn Feasts and examine whether there is a development towards the Feast of Tabernacles being the great Feast of Harvest. Let's also ask ourselves whether here, too, there is a climax on the last Great Day and the Final Day of the Feast of Tabernacles. And, finally, let's consider the prophetic significance of the Autumn Feasts.

---

[a] Leviticus 23:23-44

5.1

The Day of Trumpets (*Rosh Hashana*)

The Day of Trumpets is one of the seven days in each year on which there is a holy assembly.[a] In contrast to all other festivals, that either start at full moon or halfway through a month, this feast starts on the day of the New Moon. The New Moon is the symbol of turning around, or a new beginning. Nowhere do we precisely find why this day is a day of remembrance. Only later in Israel's history was this day taken for the 'birthday of the world'. This explains why many people believe God began his Creation on that day.[148]

Because of this day of the coronation of creation, a joyful noise with the trumpet was made before God the King.[b] From the point of view of collectivity, to celebrate the birthday of creation binds up the individual with all of creation on the one hand, and creation with all of mankind on the other. New Year's Day falls in the seventh month, with six months behind us and another six months ahead. With God, both the end and the beginning of the year are bound up in the middle of the year. The middle or the centre of the year is also called the 'head of the year', '*Rosh Hashanah*'.

In addition to the ram's horn, or shofar, silver trumpets were used on this day.[c] Silver is not only a form of payment for settlements or reconciliation, but also the sign of a soul's redemption[d][149] Only after redemption could the people enter the rest of the Sabbath and the festivals.[e]
The Day of Trumpets is therefore a day of repentance, of spiritual preparation for the Sabbath.[f]
The trumpet is meant to announce the Day of Atonement, ten days later.[150]

---

[a] Leviticus 23 [b] Psalm 98:6 [c] Numbers 10:2; Psalm 98:6
[d] Exodus 30:11-16 [e] Matthew 1:28-30; Hebrews 4:1-11
[f] Leviticus 23:23

The ten days from the Day of Trumpets to the Day of Atonement are days of repentance and self-examination, '*Heshbon Ha-Nefesh*', or '*Aseret Yomei Teshuva*'. These awesome days, also called '*Yamim Noraim*', are celebrated with joy, to express confidence about the future.[151] By examining yourself you can face up to your own failures, without having fear of being banished from the community. This teaches us that the community will only function if everyone takes his place. The reading on this first day emphasizes solidarity with mankind.[a] And each day, up to the Day of Atonement, Psalm 27 is read twice, since the closing of Psalm 27 is a call to wait upon the Lord.

The Day of Trumpets announces not only the Day of Atonement, but also a wedding feast.[152] We already came across the image of a marriage at Passover.
Certain customs were practised at weddings. In the times of the Israelites, when a man wanted to get married, he would go to the father of his beloved to arrange a marriage contract. Then he would leave to prepare a bridal room for his bride. About two years later, after finishing the room, he would return to 'steal' his bride, as a 'thief in the night'. He would take her to his bridal room for seven days, after which he would return to celebrate the wedding feast with the guests.

The Autumn Feasts are also interpreted as Harvest Feasts. From a historical point of view, the Israelites were taught to celebrate Passover, when they were still in Egypt. During the journey out of Egypt they celebrated two feasts: Unleavened Bread and Shavuot. But it was not until they had entered the Promised Land that they could really celebrate the Harvest Feast[b] [153]

A great tragedy occurred at Kadesh-Barnea, which means 'Unwilling Son', when the Israelites refused to listen to the spies and enter the Promised Land, and thus celebrate the great Harvest Feast. It was only after forty

---

[a] Genesis 21:1-34 [b] Numbers 13-14

years that the next generation could enter the land and celebrate the Harvest Feast;[a] it took a long time of preparation before they were finally able to celebrate the Harvest Feast. In present-day Israel this lengthy time of preparation is commemorated by the fact that preparations for the Autum Feasts start forty days in advance – from the 1st Elul up to the 10th Tishri, the Day of Atonement. These forty days of repentance, *'Teshuva'*, are to be used for returning to God and being reconciled with God and one's fellow-men.[b]

Within Jewish liturgy, The Day of the Trumpets or Rosh Hashanah has acquired the meaning of 'establishing the Kingdom of God'. In the desert, the Israelites were on their way to becoming a holy nation, a 'kingdom of priests'.[c] *Rosh Hashanah*, therefore, is also *'Yom HaZikaron'*, a Day of Remembering this commission. The Day of Trumpets is also called the Day of Judgement, returning to God, *'Teshuva'*, the focus of the people's minds.[154] The Talmud says that on this day God rises from the judgement throne and sits down on the throne of grace.[155] This is a reference to the Day of Atonement.

The Day of Trumpets marks the beginning of the Autumn Feasts and is thus chiefly future-oriented: it announces the ten days of repentance, the Day of Atonement, and the Messianic wedding feast.
In the NT, this image of a wedding feast with a bride and bridegroom becomes an image of Jesus and his church,[d] which includes Jews and Christians. He has made the two into one church. With his blood, the bridegroom signs the contract of the New Covenant.[e] After that, Jesus goes to heaven to prepare a place for his bride.[f] And one day He will return to celebrate, with his Bride, the Great Wedding Feast.[g]

---

[a] Joshua 5:10; Leviticus 23; Nehemiah 8; [b] Leviticus 23 [c] Exodus 19:6
[d] Ephesians 2:15 [e] Mark 14:24 [f] John 14:2,3 [g] Revelation 19:7-8

5.2

The Day of Atonement (*Yom Kippur*)

The Day of Atonement is the most important Sabbath of the year. Between *Rosh Hashanah* and the Day of Atonement there are ten days of repentance, ten days for confessing one's sins, '*Viddui*', and making up with God.[a] On the Day of Atonement, or '*Yom Kippur*', the focus is on the notion '*kappara*', reconciliation. Therefore, this is the central day of national reconciliation and purification.

We can conclude from the Feast Calendars that there are precisely three times forty days between *Shavuot* and *Yom Kippur*, or between the first time the Ten Words were given and the second time. God has issued very precise instructions on how a person may be reconciled on this Day of Atonement.[b] The high priest must take off his eight special garments in order to fulfil his task as an ordinary priest, clothed in linen.[c] [156]

In addition to the forty acts that the high priest is to perform on this day,[157] he must call out the Name of the Lord ten times: six times in connection with the bull, three times for the scapegoat, and once for the lot. People hearing the Name must throw themselves down to the ground, in awe of God.

Throughout the Feasts of the Lord, there is a development towards the centre of service to God, the centre being the altar.[158] This development can be observed as follows.

At Passover, only the door posts were sprinkled seven times; at the Feast of Weeks, the people and the Book of the Law were sprinkled seven times, and now, on the Day of Atonement the altar in the sanctuary is sprinkled seven times.

---

[a] Leviticus 16:29-31; 23:27-32 [b] Leviticus 16
[c] Leviticus 8:7; Exodus 28:27-32

The altar is also called 'the throne of grace' At 'the throne of grace', the atonement cover on the ark, the high priest comes nearer than ever to God's presence, the Shekinah or the glory of God.

The prophet Daniel also speaks of a day of cleansing of the sanctuary and the altar.[a] Hence the altar, which occupies centre stage on this day, is important in the service to God.
Now that the altar is no longer present, people pray for Israel's redemption.[b]

The following prophecy refers to the Day of Atonement, "I will remove the sin of this land in a single day."[c] Will this happen on some future Day of Atonement? It will be after the days of repentance that God himself will come to cleanse them.[d] From a prophetic point of view, will this be after the days of repentance?

On the Day of Atonement, two passages are read from the Torah, 'Parashot', i.e. Leviticus 16-18 and Leviticus 19-20, in which the reconciliation (Leviticus 16) is linked to the resolving of conflicts between people (Leviticus 19). The restoration of the relationship between God and man has consequences for interhuman relationships.

The reading from the Prophets comes from Hosea 14, and deals with reconciliation after repentance. The extra feast scroll on this day is the book of Jonah.[159] The central theme of this book is repentance, both individual (for oneself) and collective (for mankind). Once again, we see the concept of the collective. At the closing of the liturgy, the prayer is that people's names may be found written in the Book of Life.[e]

In the three-year cycle, Genesis 32-33 is read on this day; these chapters deal with Jacob's struggle at the Jabbok and his reconciliation with Esau, as a foreshadowing of the Day of Atonement.[160] At the end of this Day of Atonement, there is the ritual of the cleansing of sins, when God hurls all

---

[a] Daniel 8:13-14 [b] See also Romans 10:1 [c] Zechariah 3:9
[d] Zechariah 12:10; 13:1 [e] Daniel 12:1

iniquities into the depths of the sea.[a] At the end, the Trumpet is sounded again.

Jewish literature mentions that God's Shekinah left the Temple forty years before its destruction in the year 70 AD.[161]
On that occasion, four signs were observed:
- The western light of the Menorah went out every night
- The lot for the Lord did not come up in the right hand of the High Priest
- The Temple door was open every morning
- The scarlet cord stopped turning white.

The priests used to bind a cord, dipped in goat's blood to the Temple's doorpost. As soon as the scapegoat had entered the wilderness, the scarlet cord would turn white again, as a sign that God had reconciled the sins.[b] The rabbis saw these four signs as God-given signs.[162] Was this an indication that God would no longer forgive the sins of his people in this way?

In Judaism, Yom Kippur is also 'Yom HaDin', the Day of Judgement. The Day of Atonement has become not only a day of reconciliation, but also a day of judgement, of separation. According to the Talmud,[163] God will open three books on this day, i.e., the Book for the Thoroughly Righteous, the Book for the Intermediate, and the book for the Thoroughly Wicked.[c] A common greeting on this day is, 'Gmar Hatima Tova', or 'May your name be inscribed in the Book of Life.'[164]   גמר חתימה טובה

On Yom Kippur, the books will be opened, but only on Sukkoth is it also called the Feast of the Opened Book.[d] [165] On Yom Kippur, man is cleansed before God and so, on this day, an end is made to God's judgements.[166]

In the NT, the Day of Atonement has been fulfilled in the work of Jesus, in that all sins have been reconciled through Him. All sacrifices point to

---

[a] Micah 7:19 [b] Isaiah 1:18 [c] cf Hoseah 14:1-9 [d] Deuteronomy 31:9-13; 16-30

Jesus' sacrifice on Calvary.[a] On the Day of Atonement, two goats were used. The goat slaughtered for the Lord refers to Christ's death. The goat for Azazal, sending away, is a symbol of Christ's resurrection which brings about reconciliation.[b]

The remarkable thing is that at Jesus' death the veil of the temple was rent, as a sign that the entrance to the Father was now open to everybody. Having suffered outside the gate, Christ is both High Priest after the order of Melchizedek, and scapegoat.[c] [167]

Just as the Tabernacle showed the people that because of their sins the way to God was not open yet and that there is forgiveness through the shedding of blood, likewise the work of Jesus shows that He is our high priest and has given himself as a reconciliation for our sins. The blood of animals could take away only physical impurity, but the blood of Jesus can take away sin itself.[d]

The Day of Atonement is the most important Sabbath of the year.
There is also a relation between the Day of Atonement and the Year of Jubilee.[e] In the 50th year, the Year of Jubilee could start after the cleansing of the High Priest, the sanctuary, and the people.
In that year, people would get back their own lands. The word 'Jubilee' also means calling, rejoicing, blowing of horns. The sound of the silver trumpet, 'Jubilee', marks the beginning of the Day of Atonement and the Year of Jubilee.[169]

The Year of Jubilee is a time of restoration.[f] The Year of Jubilee is prophetically present in the work of Christ during his first preaching at Nazareth, where He proclaims the year of the LORD'S favour, the Year of Jubilee.[g] This is the year of homecoming for the homeless.

---

[a] Hebrews 1:204; 3:3-6; 7:26-28; 8:1-6; 9:23; 10:1-12 ; Daniel 9:27
[b] Colossians 2:13; 3:13; John 1:9 [c] Galatians 2:20; Hebrews 8-9
[d] Hebrews 9:11-14 [e] Leviticus 25:35-55 [f] Acts 3:19-21 [g] Isaiah 61

The silver trumpet was blown at the end of the Day of Atonement. This indicates that after the struggle, victory can be celebrated,[a] and people may enter the rest of the Year of Jubilee.[b] In this way, the Day of Atonement refers to the coming of the Messiah who will come to gain the victory, to reconcile, and to restore – so that the Year of Jubilee can begin.

Yom Kippur at the *Kotel*, Jerusalem

---

[a] Joshua 6   [b] Leviticus 25:10-54

5.3

The Feast of Tabernacles (*Sukkoth*)

The Feast of Tabernacles is the last and great feast of the Autumn Feasts. It is celebrated in the seventh month,[a] and is also known as the Feast of Ingathering, '*Chag Ha-Asif*'.[b] This Ingathering is the name of the Fruit Harvest, at the end of the year.[169] It is also called 'Feast of Tabernacles' because of the fact that the Israelites lived in 'tabernacles' or booths during their 40-year journey through the desert.[c] [170]

Yet another name for this feast is 'Festival to the Lord',[d] or 'Feast in the seventh month', which suggests fullness and completion.[e] And in the context of the history of salvation, it is called 'the Great Feast'.[f]

In brief, this feast is a harvest feast as well as a pilgrim feast with a prophetic purpose.[171] It is difficult to discover its original meaning from the feast calendars. As we have seen, it is highly probable that the notion of remembrance became intermingled with agricultural influences. A certain development can be discovered in the history of the Feast of Tabernacles, which runs parallel with that of the Israelites who first lived in tents in the wilderness, and only later, in the Promised Land, in houses.

The tabernacle, too, was first the tent of God, and only later did the Temple come to be the house of God. This may be a reflection of the fact that living in tabernacles or tents is living under God's protection, and, ultimately, living in the house of the LORD.[g] Here, the earthly tabernacle would be an image of the heavenly tabernacle.[h]

The Book of Jubilees says Abraham is the founder of the Feast of Taber-

---

[a] Leviticus 23:33-34 ; Deuteronomy 16:13; Zechariah 14:16; Ezekiel 3:4

[b] Exodus 23:16; 34:22; [c] Deuteronomy 16:13; Leviticus 23:34

[d] Numbers 29:12; Judges 21:19 [e] Nehemiah 8:14 [f] 1 Kings 8:2; Ezekiel 45:25
 Nehemiah 8:14; Hosea 12:9; Psalm 81:1-3 [g] Psalm 27:4-6

[h] Hebrews 8:2,5

nacles.[a] Abraham lived in tents, as did Isaac and Jacob, for he was looking forward to the city built by God.[b] This is an early indication of the feast's prophetic significance.

People celebrate this feast to be reminded of the fact that the Israelites lived in booths during their journey through the wilderness. Booths are a reminder that the Israelites lived on earth as foreigners and aliens. The booth or Sukkah is a taste of the world to come, 'Olam Haba'.[172]

In the world to come, the righteous will get a *Sukkah* – this is the bridge between Paradise and the World to Come, retrospective and perspective, past and future: the bridge to God's throne.[173]

It is possible to compare Abraham – who left Ur and lived in a tent in the Land of Promise – and Aaron – who spent seven days in the entrance of the tent of God, before he was ordained high priest on the eighth day. The Sukkah is compared with God's canopy, a baldachino, to celebrate the marriage between God and his people. Sukkoth is the Great Feast, at which people meet their God, in their tents or homes. However, they keep yearning for the great day on which God will come to live with his people.[c] During the journey through the wilderness, the tabernacle was God's booth or tent.

Later David took the tabernacle to Jerusalem. During the reign of King Solomon the Temple was dedicated as the House of God.[174] It took seven years to complete building the Temple. Its dedication took place during the Feast of Tabernacles in the seventh month.[d]

'The Feast' had to be celebrated 'between the evenings', presumably 'in the evening when the sun goes down'.[e]

The phrase may also indicate the time for the evening sacrifice.[175]

From the evening of the 14th day, i.e., from the beginning of the 15th day, this Feast had to be celebrated, that is, at Full Moon.

'The Feast' had to be celebrated night and day, with the gates of the Tem-

---

[a] Jubilee 16:26 [b] Hebrews 11:9-10 [c] Isaiah 33:20-24
[d] 2 Chronicles 5:3; 1 Kings 8:1-2 [e] Deuteronomy 16:6

ple opened at all times. Because of the lighting of four large candle
-stands, there was sufficient light on the Temple Square during the night
for the celebration of 'the Feast'.[176]

A special characteristic is that 'the Feast' lasted for seven days, from the
15th up to the 21st of the seventh month. It was then followed by an extra
Sabbath on the eighth day of 'the Feast', the 22nd of the month.[a] On this
extra Festive Day, people prayed for rain for the next season.[b] Rain is a
token of God's blessing in the Promised Land.[c] It speaks of refreshment
and renewal.

The Lord promised to bless with grain, wine, and oil in the spring and
autumn harvests.[d] The seven crops or fruits are barley, wheat, grapes, figs,
pomegranates, olives, and dates.[e] The barley harvest starts at Passover, the
wheat harvest ends at *Shavuot*. At *Sukkoth,* the other fruits were brought to
the Temple. Five of the seven fruits of the Promised Land are tree fruits
(grapes, figs, olives, dates and pomegranates). The OT frequently writes
about the wine of grapes. The fig tree is the image of the Torah, of which
a little bit is picked every day. The pomegranate adorned the Temple and
the garment of the high priest. Only after many years will the olive tree
bear fruit in abundance. The produce of all these fruit trees is harvested at
Sukkoth. That's why *Sukkoth* is the Great Harvest Feast.

There are very detailed prescriptions for this Feast of Tabernacles, during
which more sacrifices were offered than at any other feast.[177]
It is remarkable that seventy bulls were offered for the seventy nations.[178]
On the first day, thirteen bulls were offered, and subsequently one bull
less each day. The Talmud recognizes this prophetic perspective, and
speaks of the seventy bulls as a sacrifice of reconciliation for the nations –
so that they too may be able to celebrate the feast.[179] *Sukkoth* is thus typi-
cally a feast for Jews and non-Jews.[f]
On the eighth day, one extra bull is offered, especially for Israel, making

---

[a] Leviticus 23:26;   Numbers 29:35 [b] Zechariah 10:1; Hosea 6:3
   [c] Deuteronomy 11:10-17; Proverbs 16:15; Joel 1:10 [d] Deuteronomy 11:14;
   Nehemiah 5:10 [e] Deuteronomy 8:8 [f] Zechariah 14

the total number of bulls offered 71. Does this suggest that Israel has a special place among the nations?

According to the instructions, the priests and Levites, at the end of every seven years, at the Feast of Tabernacles, were to take the Book of the Covenant out of the Ark and read passages from it to the Israelites, for the sake of explanation.[a] [180] This was not done on any of the other feasts, Passover and *Shavuot.*

This is a clear indication of the pivotal role of Sukkoth. Since the second period of the Temple the Torah is divided throughout the year, with the Torah readings for *Sukkoth* being:[181]

1. Both first two days: Leviticus 22:26-23:44
   The first day: Prophets/Haftarah, Zechariah 14:1-2 and Writings, Psalm 105
   The second day: Prophets/Haftarah, 1Kings 8:2-21 and Writings, Psalm 29
2. The intermediate days: Torah, Numbers 29:17-34 and Writings, Psalm 50:16ff, Psalm 94:16ff, Psalm 94:8ff, Psalm 81:6ff, Psalm 82:5ff
3. Sabbath: Torah, Exodus 33:12-34:26
   Prophets/Haftarah, Ezekiel 38:18-39:16
4. The seventh day: Torah, Deuteronomy 14:22-16:17
   Prophets/Haftorah, 1Kings 8:54-9:1
5. The eighth day: Torah, Deuteronomy 33:1-34:12 and Genesis 1:1-2:3
   Prophets/Haftorah, Joshua 1:1-18

It is illustrative that the Torah has a specific instruction for the Feast of Tabernacles, Sukkoth, namely that participants must have complete joy before God's countenance, *'Zeman Simchatenu'.*[b] It is like an extra commandment, 'Rejoice before the Eternal One'[c] and 'Be joyful'.[d]

At the conclusion of *Sukkoth,* the Torah cycle of lectures is rounded off

---

[a] 2 Chronicles 17:7-9; Malachi 2:1-10 [b] Deuteronomy 16:15
[c] Leviticus 23:40 [d] Deuteronomy 16:14

with the Rejoicing in the Law, *Simchat Torah*, and is immediately restarted with the reading of Genesis 1. As the Word of God remains effective as the source of all life, life goes on. This is symbolized in the readings about the beginning of all life in Genesis 1.

On this day the reading from the Prophets is taken from Joshua 1. Having taken over the leadership from Moses, Joshua conquers the land to fulfil God's promise of land to the Israelites. For this reason, Sukkoth was not celebrated until the Israelites had entered the Promised Land, as a sign of a new season or era. Joshua is instructed to keep observing the Torah. And so every generation should continue observing the Torah and take up its responsibility. At *Sukkoth*, the great harvest has been taken in and the year can start anew.

In addition to the Torah readings, the book of the Preacher was read as the feast scroll during this Feast of Tabernacles. To the Preacher, a booth is the correct metaphor for life: unpredictable in every way, apart from the certainty that God is our heavenly protection. The *Sukkah* was made of branches of the palm, willow, myrtle, and olive, as a sign of victory, weeping, rejoicing, and anointing.

Passages were read from both Ecclesiastes and Proverbs 22 about the fact that rich and poor alike are made by God and that both should celebrate before God's countenance.[a] Poor people, widows, Levites, and aliens shared the blessing at this Greatest Feast of the year.[b] Doing justice to the poor, by sharing the harvest, is righteousness, an act of charity, '*Tzedaka*'.

Well before the Exile, Isaiah prophesied about the Great Feast at which the finest of wines would be served.[c] It is highly probable that he was referring to the Feast of Tabernacles, which takes place when the grapes have been harvested. Furthermore, in the image of the *Sukkah*, the prophet Isaiah outlines the future for Jerusalem: it will be like a peaceful abode, a tent that will not be moved when the Lord will save his people.[d] However, God's people did go into Exile first, particularly because of the

---

[a] Psalm 100 [b] Deuteronomy 16:9-16 [c] Isaiah 25:6-8 [d] Isaiah 33:20-22

way in which they dealt with the feasts. God began to hate their way of celebrating them.[a] After the Exile, the *Sukkah* became a sign of the frailty of life cut off from its natural centre, i.e. the land of Israel.

Erecting the *Sukkah* then became a prayer for national autonomy and for the coming of the Messiah who will redeem the world.[182] Isaiah prophesied that Jerusalem will be like a tent that will not be moved, in which God will be both Judge, Lawgiver, and King.[b] This perspective of the Kingdom of God even indicates that one day the people will be justified from all their transgressions. (See the NT perspective that all Israel will be saved and justified.)[c]

The later OT books (Ezra, Nehemiah, Haggai, and Zechariah) frequently speak about this Feast of Tabernacles.
In Ezra's time, the Feast of Tabernacles was still celebrated without the Temple. First, the altar for burnt offerings was restored.[d]
The Torah was read in its entirety. In Sabbath Years, when there was no harvesting,[e] people would focus particularly on the reading of the Torah.[f] After the building of the Temple, with Nehemiah, the Feast of Tabernacles was celebrated again.

The books of Ezra and Nehemiah deal with the restoration of the people from Babel, the restoration of Jerusalem and the Temple, and with the Feasts of the Lord. All the people assembled as one man from all parts of Israel in the square before the Water Gate.[g]
They drew water from the Pool of Siloam for the sacrifice, and brought it to the Temple, through the Water Gate. And they opened the Book of the Law and read from it, as a reference to Moses striking water from the rock.
Thus the Feast of Tabernacles has become the Feast of the Opened

---

[a] Isaiah 1:11-16;   Isaiah 5:11-12; Isaiah 28:7-8;   Jeremiah 51:37-39
   Lamentation 1:4; 2:6-8; 22; Hosea 2:8-11; 9:3,5 ;   Amos 5:21-24; 8:10
   Malachi 2:1-3,7-10 ; Zechariah 7:5-15 [b] Isaiah 33:20-24
   [c] Romans 11 [d] Ezra 3:6-7 [e] Deuteronomy 31:10 ff
   [f] Ezra 3:4; Nehemiah 8:19 [g] Nehemiah 8:1

Book.[183] The people built booths, and their joy was very great.[a]

The prophets Haggai and Zechariah also summoned the people to continue rebuilding God's Temple, despite opposition.[b] In this respect, the deeper meaning of the name Haggai is revealing; it means 'Chag', feast or born during a feast. He summoned the people to complete, first of all, the house of God, so that autumn and spring rains would come, as well as a fine harvest.[c] Haggai's prophecy that the glory of this present house will be greater than the glory of the first house (the temple), is expressed on the 21nd day of the seventh month,[d][184] the final day of the Feast of Tabernacles.[185]

That is the reason why the glory of God as expressed in (CH) the first and second Temples is bound up with the Feast of Tabernacles.
Will the future glory of God also come during the Feast of Tabernacles?[186]

Partly because of Haggai's prophecy, the Feast of Tabernacles has become the Greatest Feast for Israel, a feast of renewing the service to God.[187] In his prophecy we see that this feast also has a foretelling nature. After the Exile, the people built the temple, but it did not turn out as beautiful as the first temple, the one of Solomon. Yet, Haggai says, this new temple will have greater glory than the former. This gives hope for the future.

The prophet Zechariah brings up this feast in Chapter 14, in which he first describes Israel's physical restoration and then its spiritual restoration. All nations are called to go up to Jerusalem and celebrate the Feast of Tabernacles. If they don't, their country will have no rain.[e] This points to the future, to the time when all nations will celebrate the Feast of Tabernacles.[f]

These days, the Feast is celebrated with the booth, the *lulav*, and the *etrog*.[188] Usually, the *lulav* is a bundle consisting of palm, myrtle, and willow branches. (Occasionally, the Israelites would take branches of olives, wil-

---

[a] Nehemiah 8:13-18 [b] Ezra 5 [c] Jeremiah 5:24 [d] Haggai 2:2,10
[e] Zechariah 14:10,17 [f] Zechariah 14

lows, and myrtles.) [a] [189]

The *lulav* refers to Israel's journey through the desert. The different kinds of branches in the bundle refer to the differences between people.[190] The sweet taste and delicious scent of the *etrog* refer to the person who knows the Torah and practises it. The myrtle (which has a delicious fragrance, but produces no fruit) is the person who studies the Torah but does not practise it. The palm branch refers to the date: it tastes good, but does not have that delicious fragrance. This is the person who acts on the commandments, but does not study the Torah.

The willow refers to the person who does neither.
In its entirety, the *lulav* symbolizes the community of Israel. People are to encourage each other and challenge one another to study and practise the Torah.[191]

Every morning, during the Feast of Tabernacles, there was the ceremony of water drawing, which started on the second evening, '*Bet Hasho'ayva*'.[192]
A priest would go to the Pool of Siloam carrying a golden jar to draw water. After a dry summer, this was the last water still on hand, from the bowels of the earth. The priest would bring this water through the Water Gate to the Temple, where he put it in a silver vessel. The water would slowly trickle out from underneath the vessel, as a sacrifice before the altar.

According to Judaism, the Water Gate has a special prophetic significance. (R. Eliezer ben Jacob equates the gate with the South Gate from Ezekiel 47.)[193] The water libation, also called '*Nisuch Hamayim*',[194] took place every morning during Sukkoth, as a symbolic prayer for rain.[195]
This custom goes back to oral tradition, Taanit 3a, and the Talmud explains this as follows, "The Almighty says, 'Pour the water on the altar during the feast, in order that the rains of that year are blessed.'"[196]

The Mishnah says that he who does not know the joy of the drawing of

---

[a] Nehemiah 8:15-18

water, has not learned real joy.[197] On the final day of the feast, the seventh day, also called *Hosha'ana Raba* because of the many *Hosha'ana* prayers, the water drawing is repeated up to seven times. The seventh and last day of the feast thus reaches its fulfilment.

Let's take a closer look at this day.
Besides the drawing of water, the lighting of lamps was another great event during the feast. Every night four big candle stands were lit on the Temple Square, causing practically every square in Jerusalem to be lit.[198]
And so the feast could continue during the night. The Feast of Tabernacles is the only feast that must be celebrated night and day. There should be no 'end' to it. The lamps refer to the *Shekinah,* the Glory of the Lord filling the Temple, as well as to the pillar of fire which was first seen during the 15th day of the seventh month. Moreover, the lamps are a reference to the people that walk in darkness and have seen a great light,[a] thus a sign of the Messiah.

Will the Messiah come at the Feast of Tabernacles?[199]

Hoshana Raba at the *Kotel*, Jerusalem

---

[a] Isaiah 9:2-6

Section 1

The Great Hoshanna (*Hosha'ana Raba*)

The last Great Day of the feast, the seventh day, is also called *'Hosha'ana Raba'*, because of the many cries for God's help, *'Hosha'ana'*. The Hallel, Psalms 113-118, is recited seven times on this special day, with the final prayer coming from Psalm 118, *'Adonai Hosha'ana'*.

Since this Psalm 118 has become the key psalm on the Feast of Tabernacles,[200] let's examine the end of the *Hallel*.[201] The *Hallel* is cited only on the first day of Passover, the eight days of *Sukkoth*, and the eight days of *Hanukkah*, as well as (after the fall of the Temple) on *Shavuot*, the eighth day of Passover.[202]

The final psalm of the *Hallel* is Psalm 118, the unrivalled, royal, Messianic Psalm,[203] which starts and ends with the same appeal, "Give thanks to the LORD, for He is good; his love endures forever."

The central part of this Psalm is formed by verses 14 and 15a, "The LORD is my strength and my song,[204] He has become my salvation (*'Yeshua'*)." And this must then be proclaimed, "Shouts of joy and victory resound in the tents of the righteous."

Three times in the Tenach we come across the words, "God is my strength and my song; He has become my salvation". It is interesting that we find these verses in the Law, the Prophets, and the Writings.[a]

A. In Exodus 15 we find the first song of God's Word, namely the Song of Moses. This song presents the whole of biblical eschatology in a nut shell: from creation, via redemption, to the Kingdom of God. According to the Talmud, Exodus 15:2 speaks specifically

---

[a] Exodus 15 ; Isaiah 12; Psalm 118

about the Feast of Tabernacles in the words, "He is my God, and I will praise Him", because we praise Him by building a beautiful Sukkah.[205]

B. In Isaiah 12 the song of victory is sung after God has once again ransomed his people from among the nations. Then, in Isaiah 12:3, we find what always takes a prominent place in the Feast of Tabernacles, "With joy you will draw water from the wells of salvation." This is subsequently proclaimed to all nations: Proclaim the song of joy.

C. Psalm 118 paints the same picture as Isaiah 12: God has his eye on both Israel and all nations. And so, at important moments, we come across the same words in the Torah, the Prophets, and the Writings. It is revealing that after every time of a great redemption the Israelites sing that God has become their salvation.

Indeed, this song of joy only occurs when there is reason for great joy, namely, when God has saved them.[a] It is revealing that the prayer 'O, LORD, save us' is said in this Psalm and that it proclaims that God has saved them.[b]

Is it a sign of sustained dependence on God's salvation? The prayer, 'O, LORD, save us', *'Hoshana'*, has become the core prayer of the Feast of Tabernacles.

To this day, *'Hosha'ana Raba'*, the great *Hoshana*, is the final day of the Feast of Tabernacles and refers to the day of God's salvation, *'Yeshua'*.

---

[a] Psalm 126:2; Ezra 6:22; Isaiah 61:10   [b] Psalm 118:14,25

Section 2

The Assembly of the Eighth Day (*Shemini Atzeret*)

After these seven days, the feast is not over yet, but is followed by another day, the final day, with an extra assembly for Israel, '*Shemini Atzeret*', or Closing Festival.[a] '*Atzar*' means to hold or hold back. We have seen that Shavuot is the Eighth Day Closing Festival, after seven days of Passover. Likewise, *Shemini Atzeret* is the Eighth Day Closing Festival, after seven days of *Sukkoth*. This eighth day is unrelated to the feast and therefore not called a feast (*Chag*), but Day (*Yom*).[206] *Shemini Atzeret* forms no part of Sukkoth; as a religious holiday it stands on the same level as the Day of Trumpets and the Day of Atonement, *Yom Kippur*. The rabbis call this separate day '*Regel Bifnay Atzmo*', a separate holiday.[207]

The seven days of the feast are part of the natural structure and conclusion of this feast. The seven-day order is well-known, as we have also seen it in the seven-day Passover Feast. The eighth day supersedes this structure. We have seen that the eighth day indicates another pattern. Does it refer to the divine order? The number eight refers to the world of miracles, renewal, the world to come.

During the seven days of the Feast of Tabernacles people are supposed to live in the Sukkah under God's protection and to learn the Torah. On the eighth day, that protection will come automatically; then the Torah will live in the people. On the *Shabat Shemini*, or 'the Eighth', Israel commemorates the fact that after seven days of preparations, Aaron and his sons were ordained in the Tent of Meeting, in which the Shekinah of God became visible.[b]

The tabernacle had just been finished. Now that Aaron and his sons have been ordained, they can commence their ministry to God. God takes the initiative by appearing himself with his *Shekinah*.[c]

---

[a] Numbers 29:35   [b] Leviticus 9-11   [c] Exodus 25:8; Leviticus 9:4

The seven-day festival is compared with the feast of a king who after seven days must take leave of his invited guests, but does not want to send them off empty-handed. The farewell gift is a small meal, the Torah, and rain for the entire year.[208]

When under King Solomon the Temple was dedicated, we see the seven-day period was too short.[a] The seven days serve to empty yourself before God. On the last day the *Hosha'ana* is prayed with great intensity.

During the feast, passages from the Preacher are read as well, in which the people are called to see everything in the light of being accountable to God. In the course of those seven days, people have actually received forgiveness, even more intensely than at *Yom Kippur.*

People really experience the eighth day as a gift of God, with the major elements being Light and Rain. These two elements again emerge in the prophecies for the future of the feast.[b][209] In the Mishnah, rain and light are also the two central elements for the people.

On the eighth and Closing Day, God sends the people home after the feast. Likewise, after the feast, King Solomon sent the people away on the eighth day.[c] According to the Mishnah, there is not a water ceremony anymore on that day. However, from *Shemini Atzeret* on, a special prayer for rain was said, '*Mashiv Haru'ach Umorid Hageshem'.*[210]

After the rabbinical debate as to whether one should pray for rain from the first day of the feast or from the eighth day, the view of Rabbi Joshua was adopted: to pray for rain only from the eighth day. [211, 212]

Praying for rain indicates sustained dependence on God. Rain is a sign of blessing, a sign that God provides what we need on our journey through life.[213]

PRAYER FOR RAIN

And it shall be that if you earnestly obey My commandments
which I command you today,
to love the LORD your God
and serve Him with all your heart
and with all your soul,
then I will give you the rain for your land in its season,
the early rain and the latter rain,
that you may gather in your grain,
your new wine, and your oil.
Deuteronomy 11: 13-14

Section 3

Rejoicing of the Law (*Simchat Torah*)

The eighth day of the feast, *Shemini Atzeret*, is also called Rejoicing of the Law, *Simchat Torah*. The first time that the name *Simchat Torah* occurs is in the 10[214] century.[214] Many of the customs associated with Simchat Torah did not originate until the 16[215] century.[215]

In Israel, *Simchat Torah* is celebrated on the eighth day. Outside of Israel, however, it is celebrated on the ninth day of the feast.[216] This ninth day is known in the Talmud as the second day of *Shemini Atzeret*.[217]

We have seen that on *Shemini Atzeret* the Torah readings are concluded. This day revolves fully around the Torah; the closing of the Torah is read, "This is the blessing that Moses pronounced", '*Zos Habrachah*'.[a]
'*Zos*', a sign of the divine, the miraculous, the essence of the world.[218]

Just as the blessings of Abraham, Isaac and Jacob were given on the three Pilgrim Feasts, likewise the blessings of Moses, David, and the Messiah are given on this day. Moses gave the Israelites the Torah, which applied to the entire assembly of Israel, and the entire Torah refers to the Messiah, who will reign on the throne of David.

On *Simchat Torah*, the end of the Torah is read. After that, the cycle starts again with the reading of the beginning of the Torah, Genesis 1. These commands are a lamp.[b] They give the joy one needs, Simchat Torah. On this day people used to read the passage about the dedication of the Temple by King Solomon.[c]

In the ninth century, a certain Rav Amram Gaon changed this reading into Joshua 1.[219] Joshua 1 is the beginning of the second part of the Tenach,

---

[a] Deuteronomy 33:1 [b] Proverbs 6:23 [c] 1 Kings 8:22

the Prophets, and thus is part of the prophetic books. The passage describes how there will be a new leader who must take possession of the land. God first mentions explicitly to Joshua that the previous period has ended. '*Moshe avdi met*', Moses my servant has died. '*Chazak we'emats*', Be strong and courageous, Joshua.[a]

God wants the possession of land promised to Moses to become a reality under Joshua. So God summons Joshua to keep the Torah. On this day, the end and the beginning of the Torah are read. The person allowed to read the end of the Torah[b] is called the *Chatan Torah*. The person reading the beginning is the *Chatan Bereshit*, while the person reading the *Haftarah* is called the *Chatan Maftir*. The word *Chatan* is a corruption of the word *Chatam*, finisher.[220] By choosing the word *Chatan*, bridegroom, there is a clear link with the marriage between God and his people.[c]

We have seen that on the Feast of Tabernacles the Hallel is recited, specifically its final words from Psalm 118.[221]
Now, on the eighth day, the circle around it is read, namely Psalm 117 and Psalm 119. Psalm 117 paints the prophetic panorama in which all the nations will praise the LORD, and Psalm 119 mentions that God's Word is a lamp to your foot and a light for your path. The lamps on the eighth day and the light of the Torah come together at *Simchat Torah*, Rejoicing of the Law. It is significant that the beginning (the word '*Bereshit*') and the end of the Torah (the word 'Israel') are both read at the close of the feast, on *Simchat Torah*. Apparently, in the liturgy for this day, Israel and the new beginning are bound up with each other. Perhaps God's Word indicates that God is busy regenerating Israel on *Shemini Atzeret*, for on *Simchat Torah* the revelation of God's Word is complete, and the joy boundless.

This is not only the day of Renewal, but also a day of carrying out Judgement. Only after the enemies have been subjected to judgement, can the victor's song of jubilee be sung.
Both Exodus 15 and Isaiah 12 are linked with the closing of the *Hallel*, Psalm 118, which is also cited on *Simchat Torah*.

---

[a] Joshua 1:6 [b] Deuteronomy 33:27-34:12
[c] Deuteronomy 32:10-14; Hosea 11:1-4

Therefore it is very likely that on *Shemini Atzeret/Simchat Torah*, the Day of Renewal, God makes a new start with his people, Israel.

On *Shemini Atzeret* one bull is offered, only for Israel.[222] On the eighth day of the Feast of Tabernacles, on *Shemini Atzeret*, the Torah is rounded off, and the Torah is opened once again. It is revealing that the last holy assembly of the people in the wilderness, the last meeting of the people in the Torah, takes place on *Shemini Atzeret*.[a] [223]

This eighth day looks forward prophetically to the last eighth day in which God will live with his people, and the Torah will be fulfilled.[b] [224]

The eighth day has a special place as an image of eternity.[225] The seven days, an image of our days, are followed by the eighth day, an image of the future. The church fathers of the fourth century took this thought as the basis for the Christian view on history. As J.Daniélou says, in the East the symbolic significance of the Biblical number seven related to the course of time of this world as a whole, and was thus in contrast to the eighth day as an image of eternity. In contrast, the West – ever realistic and historical in its viewpoints – has looked for an image of the succession of periods in the same number seven.[226]

In the first few centuries there were two different schools of thought when it came to the interpretation of time. The School of Alexandria, being familiar with the allegory, explained the seven days as the present dispensation, and the eighth day as the future dispensation. However, the School of Antioch, being familiar with real explanation, disagreed with this view and saw time as ordered in seven periods, the Millennium Age being the seventh period. And so the Church of the East has regarded the number seven as a picture of fullness, and the number eight as one of the future. The Church in the West has ordered time in seven periods, but from Augustine on, that view underwent some change. It was Basil the Great who considered Sunday the first day of the renewal, a day with a prophetic dimension. The discontinuity was necessary to indicate that something new was needed.

---

[a] Numbers 29:35-40   [b] Numbers 29:35-40

In contrast to this, Gregory of Nazianzus argued that the eighth day was an extension of what preceded. The Cappadocians in the fourth century, and later Augustine, tried to make a synthesis of this. It was Augustine who made a connection between the Eighth Day, also called the first day of the week, and the Day of the Lord.[227]

J.Daniélou indicates that the symbolism of the week was regarded as a religious interpretation of history.[228] The number seven is important for the ordering of time in days and years. The seventh day is a Sabbath, a day of rest. The seventh year is a Sabbath year, in which the land received rest. But an extra year, the eighth year, was needed for the Year of Jubilee, the 50th year, beside the 7 x 7 years. This addition has something to do with the future.[229]

The Sabbath is the image, the typology, of time. When the Day of the Lord appears, it will be an eternal Sabbath. The Sabbath is the image of rest: ceasing to work, and especially ceasing to sin. With that, the Sabbath is the future image of time and history.[a] [230]

As we have seen with Athanasius, Pentecost – the ultimate culmination of Passover – is also an image of the Day of the Lord. The 50-day period is an image of the future world. As Pentecost coincides with the Day of Resurrection, the Feast of Pentecost is linked with that eighth day of the future. The church fathers did see the symbolism in the day of Pentecost, as a closing of Passover, but did not know the closing of the Autumn Feasts in *Shemini Atzeret*.

Shemini Atzeret, Closing of the eighth day, has a further reference to the eighth day of the future. This day is a prophetic day in God's plan of salvation. *Shemini Atzeret* is still waiting for its final fulfilment.

---

[a] Isaiah 1, 13-17; 63:13

5.4

'The' Feast according to Christ

Jesus frequently refers to the Feast of Tabernacles. Let's take a look at the major references. It is quite likely that Jesus was born in a sukkah at Bethlehem.[231] The coming of Christ is described as the tabernacling of the Word of God among us.[a] [232] The association with *Sukkoth* is obvious. *Sukkoth* is the best demonstration of the fact that God wants to live with us through the Messiah.[233] If Jesus was born during *Sukkoth*, this could mean He was brought to the Temple eight days later to be circumcised, possibly during *Shemini Atzeret*.

We know that the priest Zechariah was serving in the Temple when the angel came to him to announce the birth of John the Baptist. Zechariah was assigned to the eighth group of Abia and served during the week of the 12th Sivan.[234] If we add the forty weeks for a normal pregnancy, we reach the 14th Nisan; this means that John the Baptist was born at the beginning of Passover. According to Judaism, the herald of the Messiah is expected in a Passover night.[b]

Jesus was born six months after John; thus we reach the Feast of Tabernacles. Nine months before this Feast, the Feast of Lights takes place, which means that Jesus was presumably conceived around the Feast of Lights or *Hanukkah* Feast. Was Jesus, the Light of the world, conceived at the Feast of Lights? We do know that Jesus did not come by chance, but He came in the fullness of time, very consciously at God's time.[c] Apparently, God's acts of salvation are inseparably bound up with his festivals.

At the Feast of Tabernacles all men from Israel would come to the Temple and stay overnight somewhere in Jerusalem or its surrounding. The distance between Bethlehem and Jerusalem is only 8 km.

---

[a] John 1:1-14 [b] Haggai 2:6 [c] Galatians 4:4

It is probable that all over the fields and in Bethlehem, booths were erected on the occasion of the Feast of Tabernacles. Jesus was born at a time when shepherds were out in the fields, which means it was probably not winter, as the sheep would have been in the stables, but rather autumn. At the end of the summer season, the shepherds would leave their booths in the fields to be used by pilgrims.

This could be a parallel between the life of Jesus and the Pilgrim Feasts.
In Israel, the eighth day highlights the Covenant between God and his people. This explains why it is a preferred circumcision day, circumcision being 'the' sign of the renewal of the Covenant between God and Israel.[235] Jesus' circumcision on the eighth day is the fulfilment of the covenant promise made to the patriarchs,[a][236] and thus gains new significance.
The eighth day of 'the' Feast is a day of renewal! The number seven points to the fullness and the number eight points to renewal, a new beginning.[237]

Jesus' core ministry was to fulfil his task in Jerusalem.
Before going up to Jerusalem, Jesus asked his disciples who He was, and Peter confessed, "The Christ of God".[b] Then, some eight days later, on the Mount of Transfiguration, Jesus' appearance changed. God was confirming that Jesus is the chosen one. The fact that Peter wanted to put up shelters or tents is a distinct allusion to the Feast of Tabernacles.[238] Peter's exclamation, "It is good for us to be here" was an expression of the belief that the Messianic age had begun.[239] To Peter, the revelation of Jesus' glory is a reference to the final rest in the future. Yet Jesus' transfiguration was only temporary, and thus holds a prophetic promise. The cloud in this passage of Scripture is a reflection of God's presence and an image of how one day God will live with the righteous.

Jesus spent the Feast of Tabernacles in a special manner.[c] He did not openly go to the feast, but secretly, incognito. Only halfway through the feast did He go to the Temple to teach the people, arriving in the middle of the feast. So He accentuated the fact that He is the centre and focal point of the feast.[240]

---

[a] Romans 15:8   [b] Luke 9:20   [c] Luke 9:28

As we have seen already, each day of the feast a priest would go to the Pool of Siloam, the sent one,[a] to fill a golden jar with water; this water had to be poured out before the altar in the courtyard.[241] During the water ceremony, the people would pray, "I will pour water on the thirsty land",[b] and sing the *Hallel*.[242]

On the last day, the Great Day of the Feast, *Hosha'ana Raba*, Jesus returned to the Temple and when the water was poured out He called out, "If anyone is thirsty, let him come to Me and drink. Whoever believes in Me, streams of living water will flow from within him".[c] Here, water symbolizes being refreshed by the Holy Spirit, who was to be poured out after Jesus' transfiguration. It is significant that Jesus spoke these words about the outpouring of the Holy Spirit during the Feast of Tabernacles. He came to the feast in secret, but He spoke these words in public, before the entire nation, as a prophecy that the Holy Spirit was to come. The OT has always connected water with the Spirit of God.[d] Jesus confirmed the OT promises that the Holy Spirit was to come.[e]

On *Shemini Atzeret*, the eighth day of the feast, Jesus said He is the light of the world.[f] The passage starts with, "When Jesus spoke again to the people, He said", which ties in with His previous observation on the living water.[g] The context of this observation is clearly that of the Feast of Tabernacles. John 8:12 indicates what happened following the ceremony of the drawing of water.[243] Lamps were lit at the Temple Square,[244] as a sign that God caused his face to shine upon his people for deliverance and hope for future redemption.[245]

The Talmud too describes a sustained process of drawing water until the lamps are lit on the Temple Square. The ceremonies of the water drawing and the lamp lighting are associated with the Exodus and the hope for a second Exodus. Just as God's *Shekinah* illuminated the people on their way to the Promised Land, light is a sign of divine activity.[246]

---

[a] John 7-9 [b] John 9:7 [c] Isaiah 44:3 [d] John 7:37-39 [e] Isaiah 44:3; Joel 12:23 Ezekiel 36:24-27; Zechariah 13:1 [f] John 7:39 [g] John 8:12

The fact that the Feast of Tabernacles is the background for Jesus' statement, "I am the Light of the world", has consequences for its exegesis. Jesus did not speak these words in the synagogue, but on the Temple Square, at the feast. Everybody could witness it. Just as the entire nation saw and followed the *Shekinah* of God, the entire nation witnessed Jesus' statement and could follow Him.[247] Jesus restored the light in the Temple.[248] Just as Proverbs says that the spirit of a man is the lamp of the LORD (NKJV),[a] the entire OT views Israel as that lamp and the NT views Jesus as that lamp. The only light that remains in Revelation is the light of the Lamb, of Jesus.[b]

We find the symbolism of the Temple lights in Isaiah, Chapters 2 and 9. It is remarkable that Jesus referred to them and declared, "I am the light of the world. Whoever follows me will never walk in darkness, but will have the light of life".[c]
On *Simchat Torah*, Jesus healed a man blind from birth, as a visible sign that He really is the light of the world.[d] Jesus sent the blind man to the Pool of Siloam, meaning Sent. In due time, Jesus himself would be revealed as the Siloam, the Sent One, the Anointed, the Messiah.[249]

What Jesus did during this Feast is a foretaste of what, from a prophetic point of view, He will do in the last days,[e] when the eyes of our hearts will be enlightened with the knowledge of God. The feast is the sign of the Enlightenment that will enable our eyes to see the light of the world.

It is noteworthy that the Feast of Tabernacles was celebrated not only during the day, but also during the night.[250] The large oil lamps would illuminate the courtyard, a place normally closed at night, but open day and night during the Feast of Tabernacles! Jesus made his statement – that He is the light of the world – at the very moment when the lamps on the Temple Square had been extinguished after the last morning of the feast. Jesus alone remains the Light!

---

[a] Proverbs 20:27 [b] Revelation 21:23 [c] John 8:12 [d] John 9
[e] Ephesians 1:17-18

During the water-drawing ceremony the priest pours both water and wine before the altar of the Lord. Compare this with what happened at Calvary, when at Jesus' death both water and blood (wine) appeared.[a]

Can this be compared with living water?[251]

The water-drawing is a sign of the separation of good and evil, which makes it possible for Israel to return to its original roots, and for the world to return to its original form (cf Genesis 1:2). Simultaneously with the drawing of water, the prayer is heard that God is going to sanctify the earth, just like the heaven. The rabbis see a similarity between the drawing of water and the water coming out of the rock in Moses' time.

We are familiar with the prophecy that there will be a prophet like Moses,[b] who will give new water from the rock.[252] This water feast is a temporary inspiration, but the Holy Spirit will give divine inspiration, as a permanent source of inspiration for prophecy.[253]

The final prophecy is that the Lamb will lead his people to the springs of the water of life.[c] As such, the Feast of Tabernacles offers a prophetic perspective on Christ's Second Coming.[254]

---

[a] John 19:35 [b] Deuteronomy 18:18
[c] Psalm 23; Revelation 7:17; 21:6

5.5

The Postponed Feast of Tabernacles (*Chanukah*)

There has been a development in Israel's history leading to an extra Feast of Tabernacles, celebrated three months later. This postponed Feast of Tabernacles, or *Sukkoth* in the month of Kislev, is better known as the Festival of Lights or *Chanukah*.[255] The postponement resulted from the fact that the Maccabees had to hide during *Sukkoth*, and were not able to celebrate the feast the way it should be. Thus they celebrated Sukkoth three months later, after their victory.[a] The Feast of the Rededication of the Temple, or *Chanukah*, is celebrated on the 25th day of the 12th month, Kislev. It focuses on the Temple and the altar,[b] and for this reason it is also called the Rededication Feast of the Altar. Josephus called it the Feast of Lights.[256]

Its origin is found in the fact that the Syrian King Antiochus Epiphanes had conquered Israel and desecrated the Temple by placing a statue of Jupiter in the sanctuary and offering a sow upon the altar. This happened on the 25th Kislev in the year 167 B.C.[c] After that it was forbidden for Jews to keep the Laws of Moses, so they rebelled, and in 164 B.C. the family of a Maccabean priest reconquered Jerusalem and the Temple. Judas Maccabee consecrated the Temple on the 25th Kislev, precisely three years after its deconsecration.[d]

During this Feast of Renewal, the *Hallel* was sung every day, and palm branches were carried in procession. The Temple was illuminated, and the candle stand stayed alight for eight days, burning on oil from a bottle that would normally last just one day. This is why the feast lasts eight days. Present-day Jews celebrating the feast at home will use an eight-branched candelabrum or *Chanukiah*, lighting another lamp every day until all the

---

[a] 2 Maccabee 1:9, 10:6-8 [b] 1 Maccabee 4:52-59 [c] 1 Maccabee 1:59
[d] 1 Maccabee 4:52-59; 2 Maccabee 10:5-8

lamps are burning.[257] Usually the candelabrum has an extra arm, the Shamash or servant light, with which to light the lamps. [258]

The Torah reading is a core element in the liturgy of the Sabbath following the Renewal Feast of the Temple. It is the reading in which Joseph makes himself known to his brothers.[a] Joseph, meanwhile, has been given a new name, Zaphenath-Paneah, Saviour of the World. Joseph is here a type of the Messiah. When his brothers went to Egypt for the first time to fetch grain, they did not recognize him.[259] During their second visit they did not recognize him either. Joseph put them to the test to see whether they had learned anything. How did they treat Benjamin? Judah was the defender here, the mediator, of his youngest brother.[260] Judah was later blessed by Jacob for his actions: he would be the first among his brothers. Throughout history, Judah has taken Benjamin's fate to heart. Joseph made himself known after Judah's plea and became reconciled with his brothers. Both Joseph and Judah are types of the Messiah. In rabbinical tradition, there are two Messiahs: Messiah ben Joseph who has already come, and Messiah ben David who is still to come.[261] It is revealing that both David and Joseph occur in Jesus' family tree.[262]

In the NT, we see that Jesus also celebrated the Feast of Lights. Specifically, the Gospel of John takes the feasts as a guideline for outlining what is so special about Jesus. The disciples wanted Jesus to make himself known to the world, during the Feast of Tabernacles.[b]
But Jesus first went to the feast incognito; only at the end of the Feast of Tabernacles did He reveal himself as the Light of the World.[c] [263] Subsequently He also showed that He is the light of the world by healing a man born blind.[d]

Following this, the Temple Renewal Feast is mentioned, which – viewed in time – was celebrated three months after the Feast of Tabernacles.
We read that during the Renewal Feast Jesus was in the Temple, walking in Solomon's Colonnade.[e] Then the Jews asked Him, "How long will you

---

[a] Genesis 45 [b] John 7:4 [c] John 8:12 [d] John 9 [e] John 10:23

keep us in suspense? If you are the Christ, tell us plainly." He answered that He had already told them, but that they had tried to stone him for it. What withheld Jesus from making himself fully known to his brothers, his people? We know that Jesus kept the feasts in order to bring them to their highest purpose.[264]

What can we learn from *Chanukah*?
The readings in the liturgy surrounding *Chanukah* tell us that Joseph was not recognized by his brothers. Even on their second visit, they did not recognize him initially. Just as Joseph in the end made himself known to his brothers, Jesus will also in the end make himself known to his people. Then the people will see whom they have pierced, and they will mourn.[a] Because of this mourning, there will be reconciliation.

It is revealing that at his death Jesus refers to Psalm 22.[265]
The beginning of this Psalm speaks of the Messiah being forsaken. Does this reference of Jesus also contain a message of hope? The Psalm ends by saying that the Name will be declared to his brothers,[b] and to a people yet unborn.[c] [266] Yet it is revealing that the crown of the Name is given to the Messiah on *Shemini Atzeret*. The reading at the Feast of Lights says that the Name of the Messiah will be made known to his brothers, Israel, under weeping. "Those who sow in tears…"[d]
Just as Joseph made himself known to his brothers the second time, Jesus will make himself known to his brothers, the Jews, at his second coming. Joseph only made himself known after Judah had taken on his role as a defender. Here the two Messiahs meet: Messiah ben Joseph and Messiah ben David.
On the last day of *Chanukah* there is also a reading from Ezekiel 37 about the reunification of Ephraim (Joseph) and Judah as the restoration for Israel!

---

c Zechariah 12:10; John 19:37; Revelation 1:7 b Psalm 22:22
c Psalm 22:31 d Psalm 126:5

It is noteworthy that Jesus went through life as the son of Joseph and that at the same time He was the son of David.[267] Jesus' first coming was incognito; people did not recognize Him as the Messiah. We have seen that Jesus went to the Feast of Tabernacles in secret.

Will his Second Coming also be connected with the Feast of Tabernacles? Is this Feast the key to understanding the Second Coming of Christ? In everything, the Feast of *Chanukah* refers to the Feast of Tabernacles.[268]

5.6

The Prophetic Significance of the Autumn Feasts

We have seen that the Spring Feasts have a parallel in and refer to the Autumn Feasts. Both their historical institution and later development have strengthened each other in this relationship. We have also seen a natural progression in the Autumn Feasts.[269] The Day of Trumpets, emphasizing conversion, is followed by the Day of Atonement, emphasizing reconciliation, and the Feast of Tabernacles, as 'the' Feast that has no equal.[270] As far as its structure goes, even the Feast of Tabernacles is oriented towards the last Great Day and the Closing Day of this feast, the days of completion and closing/renewal of all feasts.

Let's now examine the prophetic significance of this for the future fulfilment.

The seven days of the Feast of Tabernacles in which the people lived in booths, show us that we are foreigners and aliens on earth – people who are looking forward to a new heaven and a new earth, the home of righteousness.[a]

The seventh day is the completion of the feast. The seventh month is the month of completion; its end refers to the beginning of the year. Likewise, the seventh feast in the seventh month is a feast of completion and a reference to the age to come. This Feast of Tabernacles rounds off the feasts, and is also a transition to the age of the Messiah.[271]

The eighth day of the Feast of Tabernacles indicates this renewal of all feasts; on this day the end and the beginning of the Torah are read.

We see that this transition from the seventh to the eighth day of the Feast of Tabernacles has great significance for the future.

---

[a] Isaiah 9:6; 2 Peter 3:13

In the Torah readings we see a relationship between the Feast of Unleavened Bread and *Sukkoth*. The text that is read on the first day of the Feast of Unleavened Bread is also read on the first day of *Sukkoth*.[a]

On the last day of the Feast of Unleavened Bread the same passage is read as on the last day of *Sukkoth*.[b] The eighth day of the Spring Feasts, *Atzeret* of Passover (*Shavuot*), can be compared with the eighth day of *Sukkoth*, *Shemini Atzeret*. Both days are the eighth day of a feast, both have a holy assembly, and both are climactic. On both days, Isaiah 12:3 is read, "With joy you will draw water from the wells of salvation."

Apparently, the Feast of Unleavened Bread refers to the redemption from Egypt, so does *Sukkoth*.[c] The Hallel is prayed exclusively on the first day of Passover, the eight days of *Sukkoth*, and the eight days of *Chanukah*. After the fall of the second Temple, it was also prayed on *Shavuot*, the eighth day of Passover.[272]

Liturgically, there is also a parallel between *Sukkoth* and *Chanukah*, through the Feast of Light. What's so surprising here is that the readings at the close of both *Sukkoth* and *Chanukah* are indeed the same, but that they take place on the seventh and eighth day, respectively.

On *Hosha'ana Raba* and on the eighth day of *Chanukah*, Ezekiel 37 is read, which deals with the restoration of Israel.

Thus *Chanukah* is connected with *Sukkoth,* but not with *Shemini Atzeret*. *Chanukah* is also the postponed Feast of Tabernacles. The day after it, *Shemini Atzeret*, is not connected to it and has an interpretation and significance of its own.

---

[a] Leviticus 22:26-23:44 [b] Deuteronomy 14:22-16:17 [c] Leviticus 23:43

Feast of Unleavened Bread	Sukkoth	Chanukah
7 days + 1 day (*Shavuot*)	7 days + 1 day (*Shemini Atzeret*)	8 days
1st day: Lev. 22-23	1st day: Lev. 22-23	
Hallel	*Hallel*	*Hallel*
	Sabbath: Ex. 33-34 & Ex. 38-39	Gen. 44:18-47:27
7th day: Ex. 15	7th day: Ezek. 37 & Ps 118	
8th day: Isa. 12	8th day: Dt 33 & Gen. 1 & Isa.12	8th day: Ezek. 37

We see that the *Hallel* is quoted abundantly during the Feast of Tabernacles. The only prayer to be uttered at *Hosha'ana Raba* is, "O LORD, save us" (Psalm 118:25). This Psalm 118 is the most magnificent of the royal, Messianic Psalms; it is found right in the middle of God's Word (OT + NT). Moreover, it is preceded by the shortest and followed by the longest Psalm.[273]

This is the order of Psalm 118:
  vs. 24 *HaYom:* This is the day …
  vs. 25 *Hosha'ana:* Lord, save us.
  vs. 26 *Baruch Haba Beshem Adonai:* 'the' prayer for the coming of the Messiah.
  vs. 27 *Shemini Atzeret:* God's light has risen.

We see a turn in the liturgy between *Hosha'ana Raba* and *Shemini Atzeret*. Between verse 25 and verse 27, we find the prophetic words, '*Baruch Haba Beshem Adonai*', "Blessed is He who comes in the name of the LORD!"

We have reached here a turning point in the liturgy

This prophetic prayer is said between the seventh and the eighth day. Does this indicate that the Messiah will come between the seventh and the eighth day? Is this the day of completion on which we pray, *"Baruch Haba Beshem Adonai"*, "Blessed is He who comes in the name of the LORD!", verse 26?

The confirmation is found in verse 27, "God has given us light; bind the sacrifice with cords to the horns of the altar." (NKJV) Due consideration is given to the altar. The Messiah will gather us around the altar so that the ministry to God can be restored.[274] When the Messiah comes, we can indeed proclaim that God's light has risen, verse 27.

At *Sukkoth* four themes are central, i.e. rain, harvest, sacrifices, and joy.

Rain is a blessing for everything that grows, and thus for the harvest.[a] Rain is not only a blessing for Israel, but for all the nations that go up to the feast. The reverse is also true: the nations that do not go up to celebrate the Feast of Tabernacles will lack rain.[b]

The blessing of rain will be withheld from people who do not observe the feasts of the Lord.

Thus the harvest passes judgement, by separating those that love God from those that do not love God.[c] God gives full joy to those that love Him.

The Lord promised to bless the nation with grain, wine, and oil at the two annual harvests.[d] Grain, wine, and oil are signs of the Word of God, the joy of God, and the anointing with the Holy Spirit. Just as the grain harvest (barley and wheat) is the key focus at Passover and *Shavuot*, likewise the fruit harvest is highlighted at *Sukkoth* (grapes and oil). The fruits are harvested at the end of the year, the harvest being a reference to the final and greatest harvest of all time.[e]

---

[a] Deuteronomy 11:13-14; Jeremiah 3:2-3; Zachariah 10:1; Hosea 10:12 Hosea 6:3 [b] Zechariah 14:19 [c] Zechariah 10:1; Hosea 6:3; Psalm 65:9-10
[d] Deuteronomy 11:14; Nehemiah 5:10 [e] Matthew 13:29-30, 36-43

Jesus is worried about the bringing in of the late harvest, before his second coming.[a] The two harvests after the early and late rains look alike, but to God they are different. We're talking here about the harvest of the just and the harvest of the unjust.[b] The Feast of Tabernacles symbolizes the late rain.[c] In the well-known words of Joel Chapter 2 we find the prophecy of the early and late rains in the first month, causing the grain harvest and the fruit harvest to coincide. Then the sower will join the mower, etc. The farmer must patiently wait until the autumn and spring rains have fallen, before he can gather in the harvest.[d] This will be a special future work of God.[e]

But the Torah already speaks of early and late rains as well, "so that you may gather in your grain, new wine, and oil".[f] The spring and autumn rains are the sign of God's Covenant and blessing, when people keep the feasts of the Lord. Prophetically, this concerns the early and the late rains which one day will come together as a double portion of God's blessing:[g]

The early rain as the symbol of the early harvest in God's kingdom, and the late rains as the late harvest for God's kingdom, the final harvest of Israel and the nations. Since one day both the early and late rains will coincide with the Feast of Tabernacles, there will also be a double harvest with the Feast of Tabernacles.

Is the fact that after the feast of the Dedication of the Temple there was an extra seven-day feast, a reference to this? Solomon's Feast of Tabernacles lasted twice seven days.[h] Is this a sign of the Messiah – that He will come at the end of the Feast of Tabernacles and that straight after that there will be another feast, to mark the beginning of the Messianic age? Can it be that after the end of this world, with the harvest of the unjust, there will be a second feast for the just?[275] Will the Messiah come to celebrate this feast that starts with *Shemini Atzeret?*

---

[a] Matthew 9:37, Mark 4:29; Luke 10:2; John 4:35 ; Revelation 14:15
[b] Matthew 25:31-34 ; 2 Corinthians 5:10; Romans 5:1-2 [c] Joel 2:23-29
[d] Jason 5:7 [e] Romans 9:28 [f] Deuteronomy 11:13-14 [g] Joel 2:21, Hosea 10:12
    Jason 5:7 [h] 1Kings 8:65

The final perspective is that the feast will be celebrated with a Messianic meal for all nations and that all nations will appear before God's countenance.[a] The words 'Holy to the LORD' will be inscribed on all bells of the horses, as well as on every pot. The words 'Holy to the LORD' will even be written on the forehead of the high priest, and all believers will be clothed in linen garments as a sign of priesthood. There will no longer be a Canaanite in the house of the Lord so that, ultimately, everything will be set apart, holy, before God.[b] Only the Holy Spirit can accomplish the ultimate purpose of this great Feast, i.e. God's holiness.[c]

The promise of the Holy Spirit in John 7 was fulfilled at Pentecost, when the first outpouring of the Holy Spirit took place on a limited number of Jews: 120. The second outpouring of the Holy Spirit on the entire nation of God will occur in the last days.[d] This immense outpouring of God's Spirit will come only when people have begun to celebrate the feasts of the Lord.[e]

Joel 2:23 says that first the autumn and spring rains will fall. Verse 28 then says that the Holy Spirit will be poured out on all people. Yet it's striking that on the day of *Shemini Atzeret* Jesus speaks about the Holy Spirit being poured out for the first time at Pentecost (*Shavuot*). The Holy Spirit will be poured out once again in the last days, specifically on Israel, and probably on *Shemini Atzeret*.

Besides being compared to a harvest feast, the Feast of Tabernacles is also compared to a wedding feast. During 'the' Feast there is the commemoration of the wilderness, the place where God wanted to be alone with his bride, his beloved nation Israel.[f 276]
In the wilderness, Israel received the Torah, the teaching of God. The Ten Words can be compared with a marriage contract. At *Simchat Torah*, after reading the end and the beginning of the Torah, the Torah, so to speak, is absorbed in its entirety by Israel.

---

[a] Isaiah 25:6 [b] Zechariah 14:16, 20-21 [c] Isaiah 2:1-5; Hebrews 13:15
1Timothy 3:15; 1 Peter 2:5-10; Revelation 19:6-14 [d] Joel 2:28-30
[e] Hosea 6:1-3; Zechariah 10:1; Joel 2:28-30 [f] Hosea 2:14-23

Thus this day has become God's ultimate wedding day with Israel, since Israel marries the Torah, the Word of God. The old Israel has violated the old covenant of *Shavuot*.[a] But God will make a new covenant with them.[b]

It is remarkable that Jesus' first demonstration of this renewing work also took place during a wedding.[c] Will the same be the case on *Shemini Atzeret*? Apparently, *Shemini Atzeret*, or *Simchat Torah*, has a pivotal place in Israel's history. Does this also apply to the nations? It is special that on this day the readings are from Joshua 1. This prophecy refers to the future in which a new leader, a prophet like Moses, will usher the nation into the Promised Land. Ultimately, Jesus will be this Joshua. After the restoration of all things, He will bring the nation into the real rest of the Kingdom of God.[d] The restoration of all things includes the completion and the renewal of everything about which the prophets have always spoken.[277] *Shemini Atzeret* is the prophetic image of that renewal and restoration, after which the Messiah can come.[e]

Finally, the Feast of Tabernacles in the month of Kislev, the *Chanukka* Feast, also indicates something of the future fulfilment. This postponed feast specifically refers to the hidden miracles or signs of God, '*Nes Nistar*', which may be important in order to get a good picture of the real Feast of Tabernacles.[278] At this *Chanukah* Feast, the Temple with the renewal of the altar takes a prominent place, and the expectation of the Messiah comes alive, the Messiah about Whom it is said, "Suddenly the Lord ... will come to his temple"[f][279]
Actually, the next is too much repetition: We have seen from the liturgy that the *Chanukah* Feast refers to the seventh day of *Sukkoth*, and thus to the completion or restoration of everything, after which the stage is set for the Messiah to come.

Jewish tradition offers us some further supportive arguments. According to this tradition, a total of three crowns are given at the feasts, as a sign of confirmation and victory:[280] the crown of the kingdom, the crown of the

---

[a] Exodus 19:5-6 [b] Jeremiah 31:31; Hebrews 8:8-11
[c] John 2 [d] Hebrews 4:8-11 [e] Acts 3:21 [f] Malachi 3:1

Torah, and the crown of the priest. The crown of the kingdom was given at Passover, when God became king. The crown of the Torah was given at *Shavuot*. The crown of the priest was given at *Sukkoth*, because Aaron had to wait for seven days at the entrance of the Tabernacle before being crowned high priest.

But on *Shemini Atzeret* there is an extra crown, the crown of the good name. This refers, first of all, to the revelation of God's good name on *Shemini Atzeret*. Secondly, the crown refers to the good deeds of God's people, so that the name of Israel becomes known among the nations. Just as the feasts of *Pesach, Shavuot* and *Sukkoth* refer to Abraham, Isaac and Jacob, likewise *Shemini Atzeret* refers to Moses, David, Messiah (as the coming of the Kingdom), to peace and to the good name for Israel. One day the Lord will make his Name known.

In liturgy God's Name is revealed on the 22nd day, as it will also be revealed in the coming world. Will this be on *Shemini Atzeret*, as a separate festive day? Then it will not be difficult to meet the commission for that day, "And your joy will be complete."[a]

We know from Jewish liturgy that though the books are opened at *Yom Kippur*, only Sukkoth is called the feast of the Opened Book.[b][281] At *Yom Kippur,* man is purified before God, and God's judgement ends.[c][282] However, God's judgement will be executed after *Hosha'ana Raba*.[283] Traditionally, *Hosha'ana Raba* is regarded as the last possibility to redeem the precepts for Yom Kippur, making repentance still possible on this day.[284]

After *Hosha'ana Raba*, after the closing of the Autumn Feasts, judgements are executed. The final day of the feast, *Hosha'ana Raba*, is thus also known as the Day of Judgement.[285] On the eighth day, the Final Day, judgement is executed and a start is made with the renewal. Because of this, the eighth day is the Day of Execution, '*HaYom*'.

At the same time, the Messiah makes a new beginning. We also find this repentance in the liturgy. Together with the ceremony of the shattering of

---

[a] Deuteronomy 16:15 [v] Deuteronomy 31:9-13, 16-30 [c] Zechariah 3:9

the *Aravah,* (sins), as a sign of salvation, the people pray, "We wait in hope for the LORD." [a] [286]

One is reminded of Psalm 126:5, "Those who sow in tears will reap with songs of joy." All this has a future perspective. Just as the *Aravah* is prophetic proof that one may live by the streams of water, the tears speak of an ultimate hope in God, Who will wipe away every tear from our eyes.[b]

In Judaism, the Feast of Tabernacles has everything to do with the coming of the Messiah.[287]

Finally, the last Bible book, Revelation, tells us about God's sanctuary and the Great Feast, the Feast of Tabernacles.[288] The ultimate perspective is that God will come and 'tabernacle' with the people which is also reflected in the structure of Revelation:[289]

> Revelation 1 deals with Christ as the great high priest.
> Revelation 4 deals with the Feast of Trumpets.
> Revelation 5 deals with the book that will be opened on the Day of Atonement.
> Revelation 7 deals with the Feast of Tabernacles.
> Revelation 8 deals with the Day of Atonement.
> Revelation 11 deals with the high priest who enters the curtain.
> Revelation 14 deals with the harvests: the early and the late harvest.
> Revelation 19 deals with the wedding of the Lamb.
> Revelation 21 deals with the Booth of God that is with men.

This last book of the Bible, Revelation, emphasizes the importance of the Great Feast, and contains an element that will be fulfilled only in the future, during the Feast of Tabernacles.[290] From a prophetic point of view, God's judgement starts with withdrawal from the world, from your house, to a place where God will protect you, to the time that God's tent will permanently be with the people,[291] Revelation 21.[292] The *Sukkah* is the sign of restored relations between God and his people, and thus offers an image

---

[a] Psalm 33:20 [b] See Revelation 7:17, 21:4

of both the lost paradise and the world to come, '*Olam Haba*' [a] [293]
With the *Sukkah*, the Great Feast has a visible foretelling nature. One day
God will come to 'tabernacle' among his people.[294]

God keeps watch over time. He will fulfil his redemptive work according
to his plan and in his time. In the same way, Jesus came in the fullness of
time. The disciples had to wait until the time of *Shavuot*, Pentecost, before
God poured out his Spirit. The disciples expected God to act soon, and so
He did at the closing of the Spring Feast.

Do we, just like the disciples, expect that God will act at his appointed
times, his festive days, his Autumn Feasts? Will God also start acting at
the closing of the Autumn Feast by sending his Son, as the Messiah and
King?[295]

כֹּל אֲשֶׁר-דִּבֶּר יי
נַעֲשֶׂה וְנִשְׁמָע

All that HaShem has said:
We will do and we will listen.

Exodus 24:7

---

[a] Zechariah 14; Revelation 21

Chapter 6

The Prophetic Significance of the Feasts of the Lord

We have put forward the idea that the feasts most probably hold a prophetic dimension. God acts in history and he himself instituted these feasts of the Lord, so that the revelation of His redemptive work in time has a connection with the festive days. The most conclusive evidence for the prophetic character of the feasts, of course, are the prophecies from God's Word, which clearly speak of the future celebration of the Great Feast.[a]

Assuming that the feasts have a foretelling nature, we have examined the prophetic dimension of the feasts. To gain insight in the feasts of the Lord, we have looked at the feast calendars, the Torah readings, and the sacrifices.

The entire Torah had to be read every seven years during the Feast of Tabernacles. Thus the entire Torah gives direction to this Great Feast. The order used for the Torah readings throughout the year, has become of secondary importance. From these readings we have seen that all feasts refer to the Feast of Tabernacles as the Great Feast.

The foretelling nature of the feasts was known in the Early Church, but has been overneglected in the course of history. Especially after Augustine, people in the Western Church began to take on a linear view of time, while simultaneously embracing the thought that the Kingdom of God had already come.

With that, every expectation of God's Kingdom in the future ceased to exist. In contrast to Greek thought, Biblical thought emphasizes the present, with a circle around it to the past and to the future.

Both the OT and the NT start from this pattern. This order of time gives the feasts another perspective. In celebrating them, people remember

---

[a] Zechariah 14 ; Revelation 7, 21

God's earlier acts and reach out to the future Messiah.

This order of time gives us a blueprint of the history of salvation as one big yearning for the Great Day of the Messiah, on which the Great Feast, with the Lord's Supper and the Wedding of the Lamb, will be celebrated. One day all the nations will go up to Jerusalem to celebrate the Feast of Tabernacles.[a] To the Jews, this feast has everything to do with the coming of the Messiah.[296]

Without doubt, there is a connecting line running through all the feasts: from the Spring Feasts to the Autumn Feasts, and within the Autumn Feasts, there is another line to the Feast of Tabernacles.

Ultimately, in the Feast of Tabernacles there is a focus on the Final Day and the Closing Day.

We have seen that throughout the Feasts there are many parallels, i.e.:
- Passover refers to God the Son.
- Pentecost refers to God the Holy Spirit.
- The Feast of Tabernacles refers to God the Father.
- *Shemini Atzeret* refers to the Kingdom of God, with the announcement of the Name of God.

This last day is important in God's history of salvation, as it foreshadows the coming century.[b]

We have seen that there is a shift in the liturgy of *Hosha'ana Raba* and *Shemini Atzeret*. Between the seventh and the eighth day of the Feast of Tabernacles, the prophetic prayer from Psalm 118:26 is recited, "*Baruch Haba Bashem Adonai*", "Blessed is He who comes in the name of the LORD!"

Is this an announcement that *Shemini Atzeret* is a special day in the history of salvation?

We think we have clearly and credibly shown that it is.

We have also found that *Shemini Atzeret* has a special meaning as:

---

[a] Zechariah 14   [b] Titus 3:7

- Closing and Renewal of the Feasts
- Closing and Renewal of the Torah
- Renewal in the Revelation of God's Name
- *'HaYom'*, the Day of Execution of all prophecies
- Day for the second outpouring of the Holy Spirit?
- Day for the complete restoration of all things
- Day for the renewal of the altar
- Day that God will wipe away every tear
- Day for the coming of God's Kingdom.

Shemini Atzeret is thus of essential importance in the history of salvation. Different views on *Shemini Atzeret* lead to varying opinions on eschatology. If *Shemini Atzeret* is part of the feast, then the completion is part of this period. This view has affected the Western church, with its seven periods of salvation history, in the course of which everything will come to completion.

If, however, *Shemini Atzeret* is detached from the feast, then the renewal cannot be incorporated in this order of time. According to the Eastern Church, time is made complete in seven periods, but an extra eighth period is needed, a time of divine intervention, in which the renewal takes place and the Messiah will come to establish his kingdom of peace. Maybe, the insight in the distinction between the seventh and the eighth day is the most important observation for our view on the future. It is clear that prophecy is not a timeless event, but the completion of God's revelation in history.[297]

Do we yearn for the ultimate fulfilment of God's purposes on his festive days, so that God's Great Feast can begin?

Appendix

Feast Cycle

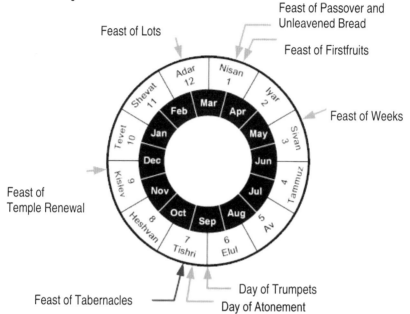

Feast of Passover and Unleavened Bread

Feast of Firstfruits

Feast of Lots

Feast of Weeks

Feast of Temple Renewal

Feast of Tabernacles

Day of Trumpets

Day of Atonement

Calendar	
Christian Calendar **Solar-year** about 365¼ day every 4 year a leap day (February 29)	**Jewish Calendar** **Moon-year** 354 days (= 11¼ day less) every 2 or 3 years a leap month (2nd Adar)

Religious Jewish year: starts on the 1st of the 1st month (Nisan)
Civil Jewish year: starts on the 1st of the 7th month with Jewish New Year (Tishri)

The seven Biblical Feasts:

o **Spring Feasts:**
   o Feast of Passover
   o Feast of Unleavened Bread
   o Feast of Firstfruits
   o Feast of Weeks
o **Autumn Feasts:**
   o Day of Trumpets/ Jewish New Year
   o Day of Atonement
   o Feast of Tabernacles (Lev. 23, Deut. 16)

SPRING FESTIVALS

Feast of Passover	Feast of Unleavened Bread	Feast of First Fruits	Feast of Weeks
Jesus' Death	Jesus' Burial	Jesus' Resurrection	Holy Spirit

AUTUMN FESTIVALS

Day of Trumpets	Day of Atonement	Feast of Tabernacles
		Jesus' Second Coming

The Three Main Feasts

Feast of Passover Agricultural: Feast of first fruits (barley) National:Out of Egypt Religious: Free from Slavery	**Easter** The Firstborn from the death Start of new life Free from slavery of death
Feast of Weeks Agricultural: First fruits (wheat) National: Start of Israel as a nation Religious: Torah given on Sinai	**Pentecost** The first congregation The Covenant for the nations The Law in the hearts
Feast of Tabernacles Agricultural: Final ingathering of fruits National: Into the promised land Religious: Inauguration of Salomon's Temple	**Prophetic** The great Ingathering Israel back to the land and to God Coming of the Messiah

Prescripts for the three main Festivals (Deut. 16: 16-17)

- Come before the Lord

- Rejoice before the Lord

- Do not come with empty hands

105

Bibliography

Abbreviations:
ICB: Internationaal Commentaar op de Bijbel, two parts, Kok/Averbode, Kampen, 2001
KV : Korte Verklaring, Kok, Kampen, 1950
TDNT: Theological Dictionary of the New Testament, 10 vols., G. Kittel and G. Friedrich (ed.);
trans. G.W. Bromiley, Eerdmans, Grand Rapids, 1964-76
WBC: Word Biblical Commentary, Word Books, Waco, 1987

****

Aalders, W., *De Apocalyptische Christus*, volgens Tenach, Septuagint en Evangelie, Uitg. Groen, Heerenveen, 2001
Adler, L., *Die Bedeutung der jüdischen Festtage*, Verlag Fr. Reinhardt, Basel, no date
Aschkenasy, Y., Over de joodse feesten, in: *Tenachon*, B. Folkertsma Stichting voor Talmoedica, Boekencentrum, Zoetermeer, 1998
Auerbach, E., Die Feste im Alten Israel, *Vetus Testamentum*, 8, 1958
Barnard, W.J., P. van 't Riet, *Zonder Tora leest niemand wel*, Kok, Kampen, 1986
Beasley-Murray, G.R., *John*, WBC, vol.36
Beek, A. v.d., *De kring om de Messias*, Meinema, Zoetermeer, 2002
Berkhof, L., *Principles of Biblical Interpretation*, Baker Book House, Grand Rapids, 1950
Berkouwer, G.C., *Dogmatische studiën*, Kok, Kampen, 1961, 2 parts
Bloch, A.P., *The Biblical and Historical Background of Jewish Customs and Ceremonies*, KTAV Publ., New York, 1980
Boersma, a.o., *Aspecten van Tijd*, Kok, Kampen, 1991
Booker, R., *Jesus in the Feasts of Israel*, Destiny Image Publishers, Shippensburg, USA, 1987
Bouma, C., *Het evangelie naar Johannes*, KV, Kok, Kampen, 1950
Braun, M.A., *The Jewish Holy Days, their spiritual significance*, Aronson, London, 1996
Brewer, D.I., *Techniques and Assumptions in Jewish Exegesis before 70 CE*, Mohr, Tübingen, 1992
Budd, P.J., *Numbers*, WBC, vol. 5
Buksbazen, V., *The Gospel in the Feast of Israel*, CLC, Fort Washington, Penn., 1954
Cole, A., *Exodus*, Tyndale OT Commentaries, IVP, Leicester, 1973
Conner, K.J., *The Feasts of Israel*, Bible Temple Publishing, Portland, 1980
Conzelmann, H., *Grundriss der Theologie des Neuen Testaments*, Mohr, Tübingen, 5th impr. printing, 1992
Conzelmann, H. and A.Lindemann, *Arbeitsbuch zum Neuen Testament*, Mohr, Tübingen, 10th impr. printing, 1991
Cullmann, O., *Urchristentum und Gottesdienst*, Zürich, 1950
Daniélou, J., *Bijbel en liturgie: de bijbelse theologie van de sacramenten en de feesten volgens de kerkvaders*, De Brouwer, Brugge, (vert.), 1964
Daniélou, J., *Sacramentum Futuri, Studie over de wortels van de bijbels typologie*, Gooi & Sticht,

Baarn, (vert.), 1993
DoVries, S.J., *1 Kings*, WBC, Vol. 12
Dupré, L., *De symboliek van het heilige*, Kok Agora, Kampen, 1991
Durham, J.I., *Exodus*, WBC, Vol. 3
Eckstein, Y., *What Christians should know about Jews and Judaism*, Word Books, Texas, 1984
Ellis, E.E., *Uitleg van het Oude Testament in het Nieuwe Testament*, IBC, 2001
Encyclopedia Judaica, XIV, col. 557-572, Sabbat, Keter Publishing House, Jerusalem, 1971/2
Epstein, I., *Geschiedenis van het Jodendom*, Spectrum, Utrecht, 1964
Erickson, M.J. *Christian Theology*, Baker Book House, Grand Rapids, Mi., 8th printing, 1991 (1983)
Fee, G., *Listening to the Spirit in the Text*, Eerdmans, Grand Rapids, 2000
Feinberg, J.E., *Walk Leviticus!*, Messianic Jewish Publishers, Baltimore, 2001
Fischer, J., *Siddoer, Messianic Services for the Festivals & Holy Days*, Menorah Ministries, Palm Harbor, 3rd ed., 1992
Gaster, Th., *Festivals of the Jewish Year*, W. Morrow, New York, 1953
Gispen, W.H., Bijbelsche Archeologie, in: *Bijbelsch Handboek I*, Kok, Kampen, 1935
Gispen, W.H., *Exodus*, KV, Kok, Kampen, 1951
Glaser, M. and Z., *The Fall Feasts of Israel*, Moody Press, Chicago, 1987
Good, J., *Rosh Hashanah and the Messianic Kingdom to Come*, Hatikva Ministries, Nederland, TX, 1989
Goppelt, L., *Theologie des Neuen Testaments*, Vandenhoeck & Ruprecht, Göttingen, 1991, 3rd printing
Goppelt, L., *Typos. Die typologische Deutung des Alten Testaments im Neuen*, Gütersloh, (1982), 1939
Goudoever, J.van, *Biblical Calendars*, Leyden, Netherlands, 1959
Graaff, F.de, *Anno Domini 1000, Anno Domini 2000*, Kok, Kampen, Netherlands,no date
Graaff, F.de, *Jezus de Verborgene*, Kok, Kampen, Netherlands, 1987
Grudem, W., *Systematic theology*, Zondervan, Grand Rapids, USA, 1994
Guthrie, G.H., *The Structure of Hebrews: a text-linguistic analysis*, Brill, Leyden, 1994
Hagner, D.A., *Matthew*, WBC, Dallas, TX, 1995, vol. 33b
Haran, M., The Passover Sacrifice, In: *Studies in the Religion of Ancient Israel*, VTSup. 23, 1972
Hartley, J.E., *Leviticus*, WBC, Vol. 4
Hayes, J.H., and J. Maxwell Miller (ed.), *Israelite and Judaean History*, SCM Press, London, 1977
Heide, A. v.d. and E. van Voolen, *The Amsterdam Mahzor*, Brill, Leyden, 1989
Henry, M., *Commentary on the whole Bible*, Zondervan, Grand Rapids, 1960
Jacobs, L., *A Jewish Theology*, London, 1973
Jenni, E. and C. Westermann, *Theologisches Handwörterbuch zum Alten Testament*, Kaiser, Gütersloh, 4th printing, 1984
Jitschak, S., *Siddoer*, vert. J. Dasberg, NIK, Amsterdam, 1986
Kasdan, B., *God's Appointed Times*, Lederer Books, Baltimore, 1993
Keil, F., and F. Delitzsch, *Old Testament Commentaries*, Reprint, Ass.Publ., Grand Rapids, no date

Kittel, G. and G. Friedrich (ed.), *Theological Dictionary of the New Testament*, TDNT, trans. G.W. Bromiley, Eerdmans, Grand Rapids, 1964-76

Klappert, B., *Die Eschatologie des Hebraërbriefs*, Munich, 1969

Knevel, A.G. (ed.), Verkenningen in Exodus, in: *Bijbel en Exegese*, Kok, Kampen, 1986 (part 2)

Knevel, A.G. (ed.), Verkenningen in de oudtestamentische Messiasverwachting, in: *Bijbel en Exegese*, Kok, Kampen, 1995

Knobel, P.S., *Gates of the Seasons, A Guide to the JewishYyear*, Central Conference of American Rabbis, New York, 1983

Kolatch, A.J., *The Jewish book of Why*, J.David Publ., New York, 1995 (1981)

Kolatch, A.J., *The Second Jewish book of Why*, J.David Publ., New York, 1985

Kraus, H.J., *Worship in Israel: A Cultic History of the Old Testament*, Basil Blackwell, Oxford, 1966

Kuiper, H., *Met Israel het jaar rond*, Kok, Kampen, 1990

Kummel, W.G., *Einleitung in das Neue Testament*, Quelle & Meyer, Heidelberg, 21st impr. printing, 1983

Ladd, G.E., *The Presence of the Future*, Eerdmans, Grand Rapids, (rev. ed.), 1974

Landman, A., *Messias-interpretaties in de Targumim*, Kok, Kampen, 1986

Lapide, P., *Het leerhuis van de hoop*, Ten Have, Baarn, 1986

Lapide, P., *Hij leerde in hun synagogen: een joodse uitleg van de evangeliën*, Ten Have, Baarn, 1983 (1980)

Lapide, P., and Luz, U., *Jezus de jood*, Kok Agora, Kampen, 1985 (1979)

Levoratti, A.J., *De interpretatie van de Bijbel*, IBC, 2001

Lincoln, A.T., *Ephesians*, WBC, Vol. 42

Longenecker, R.N., *Biblical Exegesis in the Apostolic Period*, Paternoster Press, Carlisle, UK, 1995

Maccoby, H., *Early Rabbinic Writings*, Cambridge Univ. Press, Cambridge, 1988

Maier, J., *Geschichte der Judischen Religion*, Herder, Berlin, 1992 (1972)

Mayhue, R.L., The Prophet's Watchword: Day of the Lord, in: *Grace Theological Journal* 6.2 (1985) 231-246

Moltmann, J., *Theologie der Hoffnung*, Kaiser Verlag, Munich, 1964

Monshouwer, D., and Vreekamp, H., *Zacharja, een profeet om te gedenken* (van Loofhutten naar Pasen), Boekencentrum, Zoetermeer, 1994

Monshouwer, D., and Hofstra, D.E., *Exodus, bevrijding door de Naam* (Pesach en Pasen), Boekencentrum, Zoetermeer, 1995

Mishnah, *Seder Mo'ed*, ed. S. Hammelbrug, Amsterdam, 1939-77

Mishnah, *Sukkah*, ed. S. Hammelbrug, Amsterdam, 1939-77

Neusner, J., *What is Midrash?*, Philadelphia (PA), 1983

Nolland, J., *Luke*, WBC, vol. 35c

Noordegraaf, A., *Leesbril of toverstaf, over het verstaan en vertolken van de Bijbel*, Kok Voorhoeve, Kampen, 1991

Noordmans, O., *Augustinus*, Bohn, Haarlem, 1952, 2nd printing

Noordtzij, A., *Ezechiël*, KV, Kok, Kampen, 1932

Noth, M., Die Vergegenwartigung des Alten Testaments in der Verkundigung, in: *Evangelische*

Theologie, 1952/3

Oegema, G.S., *De Messias in talmoed en midrasj*, Ten Have, Baarn, 1993

O'Higgens, P. and N., *Good News in Israel's Feasts*, Reconciliation Outreach, Stuart, Florida, USA, 2003

Oort, J. van, *Augustinus, facetten van leven en werk*, Kok, Kampen, 1989

Oort, J. van, *Jeruzalem en Babylon*, 1987, 3rd printing, Boekencentrum, Den Haag

Ouweneel, W.J., *Hoogtijden voor Hem, de bijbelse feesten en hun betekenis voor Joden en christenen*, Medema, Vaassen, 2001

Pawson, D., *When Jesus Returns*, Hodder & Stoughton, Londen, 1995 (2001)

Pentecost, J.D., *Things to Come, A Study in Biblical Eschatology*, Zondervan, Grand Rapids, 1964 (1958)

Petuchowski, J.J., in: *Vetus Testamentum* 5, 1955

Petuchowski, J.J., *Van Pesach tot Chanoeka: de wereld van de joodse feesten en gebruiken*, Ten Have, Baarn, 1986

Poot, H., *Jozef, een messiaanse geschiedenis*, Novapres, 1998

Poll, E. v.d., *De feesten van Israel*, Shalom Books, Putten, 1997

Pop, F.J., *Bijbelse woorden en hun geheim*, Boekencentrum, Den Haag, 1964

Reiling, J., *Het Woord van God, over Schriftgezag en Schriftuitleg*, Kok, Kampen, 1987

Ridderbos, H.N., *Mattheüs*, KV, Kok, Kampen, 1952 (2nd printing)

Ridderbos, H.N., *Paulus, ontwerp van zijn theologie*, Kok, Kampen, 1971, 2nd printing

Riet, P. van 't, *De invloed van het Jodendom op de Westeuropese cultuur*, Stichting Judaica Zwolle, Zwolle, 1992

Robertson, A.T., *A Harmony of the Gospels*, Harper and Row, New York, 1922

Roukema, R., *Het gebruik en de uitleg van de Bijbel in de eerste eeuwen van het christendom*, IBC, 2001

Ruler, A.A. van, *Over de Psalmen*, Callenbach, Nijkerk, 1983 (2nd printing)

Ruler, A.A. van, *Marcus*, Kok, Kampen, 1972

Runia, K., *Van feest tot feest steeds voort*, CeGeBoek, 1999

Sacks, S., *Hebrews through a Hebrew's eyes*, Lederer Messianic Publ., Baltimore, 1995

Scarlata, R., and Pierce, L., *A Family Guide to the Biblical Holidays*, Christian Press, Madison, 1997

Schauss, H., *The Jewish Festivals*, Pantheon Books, N.Y., 1996 (1938)

Scholem, G.G., *Major Trends in Jewish Mysticism*, Schocken Books, New York, 1974 (1946)

Siebesma, P.A., *Tussen Jodendom en Christendom*, Kok Voorhoeve, Kampen, 1996

Schnackenburg, R., Die Kirche als Bau: Epheser 2:19-22 unter ökumenischem Aspekt. In: *Paul and Paulinism*, ed. M.D. Hooker and S.G. Wilson, London, S.P.C.K., 1982

Shachar, I., *The Jewish Year*, Brill, Leyden, 1975

Siertsema, B., (ed.), *Visioen en Visie, het boek Openbaring – uitleg en viering*, Kok, Kampen, 1999

Smith, R.L., *Micah-Malachi*, WBC, vol. 34

Soetendorp, J., *Symboliek der Joodse Religie*, BZZTOH, Den Haag, 1990 (1958)

Soggin, J.A., *An Introduction to the History of Israel and Judah*, SCM Press, Londen, 1993 (vert. J.Bowden)

Stern, D.H., *Jewish New Testament Commentary*, JNT Publ., Clarksville, 4th printing, 1995

Stern, Y., *The Three Festivals, Ideas and Insights of the Sfas Emes on Pesach, Shavuos and Succos*, Mesorah Publ., New York, 1993

Stock, *Handboek voor de Bijbelse Geschiedenis*, Voorhoeve, Den Haag, 7th printing

Strack, H.L., and P. Billerbeck, *Kommentar zum Neuen Testament aus Talmoed und Midrasch*, Beck, Munchen, Bd. 2, 1978 (1922-28)

Thieberger, Fr., *Jüdisches Fest, jüdischer Brauch*, Athenäum Verlag, Königstein, 3rd printing, 1985 (1937)

Thiessen, H.C., *Lectures in Systematic Theology*, (revised by V.D.Doerksen), Eerdmans, Grand Rapids, 1997 (1949)

Teeffelen, P.J.M. van, *De moderne dagen van Noach*, Chr.uitg. Initiaal, The Hague, 998

Urbach, E.E., *The Sages, Their Concepts and Beliefs*, Harvard Un. Press, Cambridge, Mass., vert. J. Abrahams, 1987

Vanistein Yaakov, Y., *The Cycle of the Jewish Year*, Jerusalem, s.a.

Vaux, R. de, *Hoe het oude Israel leefde*, Boekencentrum, Den Haag, 1986 (1973)

Voolen, E. van, *Joodse feestdagen*, Kok, Kampen, 1987 (5th printing)

Vorst, I., e.a., *Badèrech, op weg naar praktisch Joods leven*, NIK, Amsterdam, 1990

Vries, S.Ph. de, *Joodse riten en symbolen*, de Arbeiderspers, Amsterdam, 1996, (1968)

Vriezen, Th.C., *Hoofdlijnen der theologie van het Oude Testament*, Veenman, Wageningen, 1987 (6th printing)

Vriezen, Th.C., and A.S. van der Woude, *Literatuur van Oud-Israel*, Servire, Katwijk aan Zee, 1989 (9th printing)

Waaijman, K., *Psalmen, bij ziekte en genezing*, Kok, Kampen, 1981 (2nd printing)

Waaijman, K., *Psalmen, om het uitroepen van de Naam*, Kok, Kampen, 1991

Watts, J.D.W., *Isaiah*, WBC, vol. 24, 25

Wenham, G., *Genesis*, WBC, vol. 1

Willems, G.F., *Jezus en de Chassidim van zijn dagen, een godsdiensthistorische ontdekking*, Ten Have, Baarn, 1996

Williamson, H.G.M., *Ezra, Nehemiah*, WBC, vol. 16

Yee, G.A., *Jewish Feasts and the Gospel of John*, M. Glazier, Wilmington, Delaware, 1989

Woude, A.S. van der, *De prediking van het oude testament, Habakuk en Zefanja*, Callenbach, Nijkerk, 1978

Zuidema, W., *Gods partner; ontmoeting met het jodendom*, Ten Have, Baarn, 1988, (1977)

NOTES

1   W.J.Barnard, P.van't Riet, 1986, 103
2   J.H.Hayes, J.Maxwell Miller, 1977, 210
3   J.Daniélou, 1993, 152
4   M.J.Erickson, 1991, 1149; W.Grudem, 1994, 1091; H.C.Thiessen, 1997, 337; J. Moltmann, 1964, 210; J.D.Pentecost, 1964, 512
5   J.Reiling, 1987, 16
6   A.Noordegraaf, 1991, 26
7   J.Reiling, 1987, 25
8   J.Daniélou, 1964, 11
9   J.Reiling, 1987, 38
10 id., 150
11 id., 33, 36
12 J.D.Pentecost, 1964, 47
13 id., 1987, 43
14 A.Noordegraaf, 1991, 15
15 J.Reiling, 1987, 42, G.E.Ladd, 1974, 324
16 G.E.Ladd, 1974, 320
17 W.Aalders, 2001, 138
18 id., 151
19 J.Reiling, 1987, 112
20 F.de Graaff, z.j., 145
21 A.J.Levoratti, IBC, 60
22 id., 41
23 W.J.Barnard, P.van't Riet, 1986, 174
24 J.D.Pentecost, 1964, 50
25 A.J.Levoratti, IBC, 57
26 L.Goppelt, 1982, 17-18
27 id., 58
28 J.Reiling, 1987, 423
29 id., 194-205
30 E.Ladd, 1974, 114
31 E.E.Ellis, IBC, 90
32 A.Noordegraaf, 1991, 14
33 J.Reiling, 1987, 42, J.D.Pentecost, 1964, 133
34 J.D. Pentecost, 1964, 60-64; L.Berkhof, 1950, 113f
35 G.E.Ladd, 1974, 322
36 W.J.Barnard, P.van't Riet, 1986, 103
37 G.E.Ladd, 1974, 111, 120
38 E.E.Ellis, IBC, 89
39 G.E.Ladd, 1974, 64
40 F. de Graaff, 1987, 302
41 W.J.Barnard, P.van't Riet, 1986, 119
42 D.I.Brewer, 1992
43 W.J.Barnard, P.van't Riet, 1986, 174
44 A.J.Levarotti, IBC, 58
45 J.Daniélou, 1964, 476, A.J.Levarotti, ICB, 57
46 W.J.Barnard, P.van't Riet, 1986, 94
47 J.van Oort, 1989, 48
48 V.Buksbazen, 1954, 26
49 J.Daniélou, 1964, 12
50 W.J.Barnard, P.van't Riet, 1986, 99, J.Levoratti, ICB, 57
51 O.Cullmann, 1950, 114
52 J.Daniélou, 1964, 29
53 A.Noordegraaf, 1991, 54
54 W.J.Barnard, P.van't Riet, 1986, 102, E.E.Ellis, ICB, 87
55 R.Roukema, IBC, 104
56 J.D. Pentecost, 1964, 22
57 R.Roukema, IBC, 109-110
58 G.E.Ladd, 1974, 243
59 R.N.Longenecker, 1995
60 G.H.Guthrie, 1994, B.Klappert, 1969
61 J.Daniélou, 1964, 16
62 id., 27
63 O.Noordmans, 1952, 18; G.E.Ladd, 1974, 64
64 No English translation found of it.
65 J.van Oort, 1987, 156, 230
66 id., 202
67 W.Zuidema, 1992, 85
68 G.E.Ladd, 1974, 64
69 A.J.Levarotti, ICB, 89

70   W.Zuidema, 1992, 86
71   A.J.Levarotti, IBC, 90
72   J.H.Hayes, J.Maxwell Miller, 1977, 210
73   H.Ridderbos, 1971, 33
74   E.E.Ellis, IBC, 90
75   W.Zuidema, 1992, 87
76   A.J.Levarotti, IBC, 43
77   B.Kasdan, 1993, 2
78   J.Daniélou, 1964, 334
79   B.Kasdan, 1993, 9
80   J.Daniélou, 1964, 314
81   E.v.d. Poll, 1997, 13
82   W.J.Ouweneel, 2001, 14, 23
83   J.I.Durham, 1987, 333
84   G.A.Yee, 1989, 70
85   W.H.Gispen, 1951, 125
86   id., 130
87   J.E.Hartley, 1992, 372
88   R.de Vaux, 1986, 414
89   P.J.Budd, 1984, 314
90   G.A.Yee, 1989, 70
91   J.E.Hartley, 1992, 376
92   Th.C.Vriezen, A.S.van der Woude, 1989,
     192
93   R. de Vaux, 1986, 414
94   R. de Vaux, 1986, 410
95   Talmoed, Mechilta Pischa, 2
96   A.Cole, 1973, 104
97   W.J.Ouweneel, in: A.G.Knevel, 1986,
     125
98   P.J.Budd, 1984, 316
99   A.Noordtzij, 1932, 468v
100 R.de Vaux, 1986, 406
101 H.J.Kraus, 1966, 46-48
102 A.Cole, 1973, 179
103 W.J.Ouweneel, 2001, 23
104 M.Haran, 1972, 290
105 E.Auerbach, 1958, 16-17
106 H.J.Kraus, 1966, 59
107 G..A.Yee, 1989, 70
108 W.J.Ouweneel, in: A.G.Knevel, 1986,
     128
109 J.D.W.Watts, 1985, 20

110 M.Henry, 1961, 828
111 W.J.Barnard, P. van't Riet, 1986,54
112 Apion 2:175
113 Mishnah, Meg.3, 4-6
114 Bab.Talmoed, Meg.29b
115 Enc. Judaica, 1971/2, 1248
116 id., 1249v
117 Yad, Tefillah 13:1
118 Bab.Talmoed, Meg.4:1-2
119 K.J.Conner, 1980, 78
120 G.R.Beasley-Murray, WBC, vol.36, xci
121 W.J.Barnard, P.van't Riet, 1986, 69
122 R.Scarlata, L.Pierce, 1997, 125
123 F.de Graaff, 1987, 32
124 W.J.Barnard, P.van't Riet, 1986, 119
125 D.E.Hofstra, D.Monshouwer, 1995, 49
126 Voor de term 'Zoon des mensen', zie
     L.Goppelt, 1991, 235v.
127 D.E.Hofstra, D.Monshouwer, 1995, 50
128 D.A.Hagner, 1995, 768
129 J.Nolland, 1993, 1045
130 C.Bouma, 1950, 81
131 D.E.Hofstra, D.Monshouwer, 1995, 59
132 W.J.Ouweneel, in: A.G.Knevel, 1995,
     101
133 D.A.Hagner, 1995, 774
134 J.Daniélou, 1964, 383
135 D.A.Hagner, 1995, 764
136 D.H.Stern, 1995, 485
137 W.J.Ouweneel, in: A.G.Knevel, 1986,
     121
138 E.Jenni en C.Westermann, 1984, 284v
139 B.Kasdan, 1993, 52
140 W.H.Gispen, 1935, 292
141 A.J.Kolatch, 1995, 214
142 Talmoed, Pesachim 68b
143 F.de Graaff, 1987, 32
144 A.J.Kolatch, 1995, 217
145 M.A.Braun, 1996, 345; W.J.Ouweneel,
     2001, 76
146 D.E.Hofstra en D.Monshouwer, 1995, 82
147 J. Daniélou, 1964, 462
148 J.E.Feinberg, 2001, 52

149 M.A.Braun, 1996, 17
150 K.J.Conner, 1980, 48
151 M.A.Braun, 1996, 28
152 A.J.Kolatch, 1995, 238
153 R. Scarlata en L.Pierce, 1997, 295
154 P.J.Budd, 1984, 140v
155 Mishnah, Yoma, 13
156 Talmoed, Rosh Hashanah, 18a
157 R.Scarlata en L.Pierce, 1997, 321
158 id., 322.
159 K.J.Conner, 1980, 77
160 A.J.Kolatch, 1995, 244
161 F.J.Pop, 1964, 498
162 Mishnah, Yoma, 67a
163 id, 39a
164 Talmoed, Rosh hashanah 1:3
165 R.Scarlata en L.Pierce, 1997, 326
166 K.J.Conner, 1980, 78
167 A.J.Kolatch, 1995, 255
168 S.Sacks, 1995, 65v
169 Enc. Judaica, 1971/2, 1443v
170 J.I.Durham, 1987, 333
171 P.J.Budd, 1984, 348v
172 A.J.Kolatch, 1995, 246
173 Talmoed, Bava Basra, 75a
174 Talmoed, Yoma, 86a
175 S.J.DeVries, 1985, 123
176 W.J.Ouweneel, 2001, 73
177 M.en Z.Glaser, 1987, 182
178 K.J.Conner, 1980, 71
179 V.Buksbazen, 1954, 49
180 Talmoed, Sukkah, 55b
181 R.L.Smith, 1984, 317
182 K.J.Conner, 1980, 71 en Talmoed, Me-
     gilta,31a
183 Y.Eckstein, 1984, 112; B.Kasdan, 1993,
     101
184 K.J.Conner, 1980, 84
185 R.L.Smith, 1984, 156
186 W.Zuidema, 1988, 143
187 K.J.Conner, 1980, 83
188 A.Noordtzij, 1932, 472
189 A.J.Kolatch, 1995, 250

190 H.G.M.Williamson, 1985, 293v
191 M.A.Braun, 1996, 108
192 M.en Z.Glaser, 1987, 193
193 A.J.Kolatch, 1995, 248
194 Mishnah, Sukkah 3.3-9
195 id., 51a
196 Babylonische Talmud, Succah 50a
197 Mishnah, Rosh HaShanah, 16a
198 Mishnah, Sukkah 5,1
199 id, 5.2-4
200 W.J.Ouweneel, 2001, 181
201 J.Daniélou, 1964, 369
202 D.Pawson, 1995, 65
203 A.J.Kolatch, 1985, 252
204 W.Aalders, 2001, 151
205 A.Cole, 1973, 23
206 Shabbat, 133b
207 F.Keil en F.Delitzsch, 720, T.Gaster,
     1953, 98
208 A.J.Kolatch, 1995, 256
209 Mishnah, Sukkah, 55b
210 G.A.Yee, 1989, 76
211 A.P.Bloch, 1980, 188
212 Talmoed, Taanis, 2a
213 M.A.Braun, 1996, 133
214 J.J.Petuchowski, VT, 5, 1955, 266-71
215 J.Shachar, 1975, 11
216 A.P.Bloch, 1980,207
217 A.J.Kolatch, 1995, 257; M.A.Braun,
     1996, 130
218 Talmoed, Megilla 31a.
219 M.A.Braun, 1996, 137
220 A.P.Bloch, 1980, 208
221 J.Shachar, 1975,11
222 B.Kasdan, 1993, 98
223 Mishnah, Sukkah, 55b
224 J.Feinberg, 2001, 54
225 id., 54
226 J.Daniélou, 1964, 369
227 id., 388
228 J.Daniélou, 1964, 397
229 id., 389
230 id., 377

231 id., 316
232 J.Good, 1989, 161
233 B.Kasdan, 1993, 96
234 A.T.Robertson, 1922, 267
235 R.Scarlata en L.Pierce, 1997, 353
236 E.v.d.Poll, 1997, 162
237 B.Kasdan, 1993, 103
238 K.J.Conner, 1980, 71
239 J.Daniélou, 1964, 480
240 id., 481
241 F. de Graaff, 1987, 305
242 G.R.Beasley-Murray, 1987, 113
243 D.Pawson, 1995, 65
244 D.H.Stern, 1995, 181
245 G.R.Beasley-Murray, 1987, 127
246 Talmoed, Sukkah 5:1
247 H.Conzelmann, in: TDNT 9:320
248 G.R.Beasley-Murray, 1987, 128
249 G.A.Yee, 82
250 K.J.Conner,1980, 88
251 G.F.Willems, 1996, 91
252 G.A.Yee, 80
253 Talmoed, Eccl.Rab.1:9
254 Talmoed, Jerushalmi Sukkah
     9a ;Y.Stern, 1993, 437
255 J.Daniélou, 1964, 491
256 Y.Eckstein, 1984, 137
257 Antiquities XII.7,7
258 Talmoed, Shabbat 21b
259 A.J.Kolatch, 1995, 264
260 G.Wenham, 1994, 389
261 Midrash, Tanchuma 44:18v
262 Zie voor de Messiassen in de rabbijnse
     traditie, G.Oegema, 1993 en A.Landman,
     1986
263 F.de Graaff, 1987, 118
264 id., 305
265 id., 302
266 A.A.van Ruler, 1983, 72
267 J.M.Mudde, in: A.G.Knevel, 1995, 58v
268 F.de Graaff, 1987, 118v
269 Y.Eckstein. 1984, 137
270 A.v.d.Beek, 2002, 289

271 M.en Z.Glaser, 1987, 16
272 A.J.Kolatch, 1985, 210
273 A.J.Kolatch, 1985, 253
274 W.Aalders, 2001, 151
275 J.Daniélou, 1964, 475
276 R.Booker, 1987, 111
277 G.A.Yee, 1989, 73
278 K.J.Conner, 1980, 52
279 Y.Eckstein, 1984, 141
280 A.E.M.A.van Veen-Vrolijk, in:
     A.G.Knevel, 1995, 200v
281 M.A.Braun, 1996, 124
282 K.J.Conner, 1980, 78
283 A.J.Kolatch, 1995, 255
284 id., 255
285 id., 247
286 M.en Z.Glaser, 1987, 198
287 M.A.Braun, 1996, 122
288 K.J.Conner, 1980, 101
289 W.J.Ouweneel, 2001, 182
290 B.Siertsema, 1999,11
291 B.Kasdan, 1993, 100
292 Targum Yonatan b. Uziel, Ex.13:20
293 M.A.Braun, 1996, 107
294 Talmoed, Bava Basra, 75a
295 M.en Z.Glaser, 1987, 212
296 P.en N.O'Higgins, 2003, 104
297 K.J.Conner, 1980, 101

INTERNATIONAL
CHRISTIAN
EMBASSY
JERUSALEM

YOUR EMBASSY IN JERUSALEM

The International Christian Embassy Jerusalem (ICEJ) was founded in 1980 as an act of comfort and solidarity with Israel and the Jewish people in their claim to Jerusalem. Today, the ICEJ stands at the forefront of a growing mainstream movement of Christians worldwide who share a love and concern for Israel and an understanding of the biblical significance of the modern ingathering of the Jews to the land of their forefathers.

From our headquarters in Jerusalem, through our branches and representatives in over 80 nations, we seek to challenge the Church to take up its scriptural responsibilities towards the Jewish people, to remind Israel of the wonderful promises made to her in the Bible and to be a source of practical assistance to all the people of the land of Israel.
For over 30 years the ICEJ has stood by Israel, showing our support in a variety of ways, both in the land and around the world. We administer several aid projects, engage in advocacy for Israel, and assist in Aliyah to the Jewish homeland.

CONTACT INFORMATION

ICEJ headquarters 20 Rachel Imeinu P.O. Box 1192 Jerusalem 91010 Israel	Tel. + 972.2.539.9700 Email: icej@icej.org Website: http://int.icej.org